TRUE
DEVOTION
to Mary

BY THE VENERABLE SERVANT OF GOD,
LOUIS-MARIE GRIGNION DE MONTFORT

A TREATISE ON

TRUE

DEVOTION
to Mary

TRANSLATED FROM THE ORIGINAL FRENCH
BY FREDERICK WILLIAM FABER, D.D.
PRIEST OF THE ORATORY

— AMERICA NEEDS FATIMA —

In this edition of Fr. Frederick William Faber's English translation of de Montfort's Treatise, meticulous care has been taken to preserve it in its original form. Thus, the English spelling and word syntax of the text, the Saint-author's extensive Latin quotations and the translator's faithful English counterparts, have all been most carefully maintained. For the sake of clarity the text has been divided up into chapters, while subtitles and layout techniques have been employed for the sake of presentation.

If you'd like to order more copies of this book, please contact:

United States:
America Needs Fatima
(888) 317-5571
P.O. Box 341, Hanover, PA 17331
ANF@ANF.org ▪ www.ANF.org

Canada:
Canada Needs Our Lady
PO Box 36040
Greenfield Park, QC J4V 3N7
844-729-6279
Info@CanadaNeedsOurLady.org ▪ www.CanadaNeedsOurLady.org

ISBN: 978-1-877905-44-5
Library of Congress Control Number: 2013940116

Printed in the United States of America

"Mary is the fruitful Virgin, and in all the souls in which she comes to dwell she causes to flourish purity of heart and body, rightness of intention and abundance of good works. Do not imagine that Mary, the most fruitful of creatures who gave birth to a God, remains barren in a faithful soul. It will be she who makes the soul live incessantly for Jesus Christ, and will make Jesus live in the soul."

— Saint Louis de Montfort

TABLE OF CONTENTS

Translator's Preface　　　　　　　　　　　　　　　　　　　xi

Preface to the French Edition　　　　　　　　　　　　　　　xv

Introduction　　　　　　　　　　　　　　　　　　　　　　　1

PART I: On Devotion to Our Blessed Lady in General

1. Excellence and Necessity of Devotion to Our Blessed Lady　　7

2. True Devotion to Our Blessed Lady: Fundamental Truths
　　　　· First Truth　　　　　　　　　　　　　　　　　　25
　　　　· Second Truth　　　　　　　　　　　　　　　　　29
　　　　· Third Truth　　　　　　　　　　　　　　　　　　33
　　　　· Fourth Truth　　　　　　　　　　　　　　　　　35
　　　　· Fifth Truth　　　　　　　　　　　　　　　　　　37

3. Discernment of False Devotions to Our Lady　　　　　　39

4. Characteristics of True Devotion　　　　　　　　　　　45

PART II: On the Most Excellent Devotion to Our Blessed Lady, or the Perfect Consecration to Jesus by Mary

5. Preliminary Observations on the Different Ways of Honouring Our Blessed Lady
　　　　· Interior Practices　　　　　　　　　　　　　　　51
　　　　· Exterior Practices　　　　　　　　　　　　　　　51

6. In What Consists the Perfect Consecration to Jesus Christ　55

7. Motives of this Perfect Consecration
　　　　· First Motive　　　　　　　　　　　　　　　　　　61
　　　　· Second Motive　　　　　　　　　　　　　　　　　62
　　　　· Third Motive　　　　　　　　　　　　　　　　　　64
　　　　· Fourth Motive　　　　　　　　　　　　　　　　　67
　　　　· Fifth Motive　　　　　　　　　　　　　　　　　　67
　　　　· Sixth Motive　　　　　　　　　　　　　　　　　　74
　　　　· Seventh Motive　　　　　　　　　　　　　　　　　75
　　　　· Eighth Motive　　　　　　　　　　　　　　　　　76

8. Figure of this Consecration in the History of Jacob Receiving the Blessing of Isaac through the Offices of Rebecca　　　81

9. Charitable Duties of Our Blessed Lady Towards her Faithful Servants　　89

10. Admirable Effects of the Perfect Consecration to Jesus by Mary　　95

11. Particular Practices of this Devotion
   • External Practices   101
   • Interior Practices   111

12. Manner of Practising this Devotion when Receiving Holy Communion 117

13. Formula of Consecration to Jesus by Mary   121

14. Preparation for Total Consecration   123

15. Prayers Recommended by Saint Louis de Montfort
   • Magnificat   131
   • Veni Creator Spiritus   132
   • Litany of the Holy Ghost   133
   • Ave Maris Stella   135
   • Litany of the Blessed Virgin Mary   136
   • Litany of the Holy Name of Jesus   138
   • Memorare   140

I t was in the year 1846 or 1847, at St. Wilfrid's, that I first studied the life and spirit of the Venerable Grignion de Montfort; and now, after more than fifteen years, it may be allowable to say, that those who take him for their master will hardly be able to name a saint or ascetical writer to whose grace and spirit their mind will be more subject than to his. We may not yet call him Saint; but the process of his beatification is so far and so favourably advanced, that we may not have long to wait before he will be raised upon the altars of the Church.

There are few men in the eighteenth century who have more strongly upon them the marks of the Man of Providence than this Elias-like Missionary of the Holy Ghost and of Mary. His entire life was such an exhibition of the holy folly of the Cross, that his biographers unite in always classing him with St. Simon Salo and St. Philip Neri. Clement XI made him a missionary-apostolic in France, in order that he might spend his life in fighting against Jansenism, so far as it affected the salvation of souls. Since the apostolical epistles it would be hard to find words that burn so marvellously as the twelve pages of his prayer for the Missionaries of the Holy Ghost, to which I earnestly refer all those who find it hard to keep up, under their numberless trials, the first fires of the love of souls. He was at once persecuted and venerated every where. His amount of work, like that of St. Antony of Padua, is incredible and, indeed, inexplicable. He wrote some spiritual treatises, which have already had a remarkable influence on the Church during the few years they have been known, and bid fair to have a much wider influence in years to come. His preaching, his writing, and his conversation were all impregnated with prophecy, and with anticipations of the latter ages of the Church. He comes forward, like another St. Vincent Ferrer, as if on the days bordering on the Last Judgment, and proclaims that he brings an authentic message from God about the greater honour and wider knowledge and more prominent love of His Blessed Mother, and her connexion with the second advent of her Son. He founded two religious congregations,—one of men, and one of women,—which have been quite extraordinarily successful; and yet he died at the age of forty-three, in 1716, after only sixteen years of priesthood.

It was on the 12th of May 1853, that the decree was pronounced at Rome, declaring his writings to be exempt from all error which could be a bar to his canonisation. In this very treatise on the veritable devotion to our Blessed Lady, he has recorded this prophecy. "I clearly foresee that raging brutes will come in fury to tear with their diabolical teeth this little writing, and him whom the Holy Ghost has made use of to write it; or at least to envelop it in the silence of a coffer, in order that it may not appear." Nevertheless, he prophesies both its appearance and its success. All this was fulfilled to the letter. The author died in 1716, and the treatise was found by accident by one of the priests of his congregation at St. Laurent-sur-Sèvre, in 1842. The existing superior was able to attest the handwriting as being that of the venerable founder; and the autograph was sent to Rome, to be examined in the process of canonisation.

All those who are likely to read this book love God, and lament that they do not love Him more; all desire something for His glory,—the spread of some good work, the success of some devotion, the coming of some good time. One man has been striving for years to overcome a particular fault, and has not succeeded. Another mourns, and almost wonders while he mourns, that so few of his relations and friends have been converted to the faith. One grieves that he has not devotion enough; another that he has a cross to carry, which is a peculiarly impossible cross to him; while a third has domestic troubles and family unhappinesses, which feel almost incompatible with his salvation; and for all these things prayer appears to bring so little remedy. But what is the remedy that is wanted? what is the remedy indicated by God Himself? If we may rely on the disclosures of the Saints, it is an immense increase of devotion to our Blessed Lady; but, remember, nothing short of an *immense* one. Here, in England, Mary is not half enough preached. Devotion to her is low and thin and poor. It is frightened out of its wits by the sneers of heresy. It is always invoking human respect and carnal prudence, wishing to make Mary so little of a Mary that Protestants may feel at ease about her. Its ignorance of theology makes it unsubstantial and unworthy. It is not the prominent characteristic of our religion which it ought to be. It has no faith in itself. Hence it is that Jesus is not loved, that heretics are not converted, that the Church is not exalted; that souls, which might be saints, wither and dwindle; that the Sacraments are not rightly frequented, or souls enthusiastically evangelised. Jesus is obscured because Mary is kept in the background. Thousands of souls perish because Mary is withheld from them. It is the miserable unworthy shadow which we call our devotion to the Blessed Virgin that is the cause of all these wants and blights, these evils and omissions and declines. Yet, if we are to believe the revelations of the Saints, God is *pressing* for a greater, a wider, a stronger, quite another devotion to His Blessed Mother. I cannot think of a higher work or a broader vocation for any one than the simple spreading of this peculiar devotion of the Venerable Grignion de Montfort. Let a man but try it for himself, and his surprise at the graces it brings with it, and the transformations it causes in his soul, will soon convince him of its otherwise almost incredible efficacy as a means for the salvation of men, and for the coming of the kingdom of Christ. Oh, if Mary were but known, there would be no coldness to Jesus then! Oh, if Mary were but known, how much more wonderful would be our faith, and how different would our Communions be! Oh, if Mary were but known, how much happier, how much holier, how much less worldly should we be, and how much more should we be living images of our sole Lord and Saviour, her dearest and most blessed Son!

I have translated the whole treatise myself, and have taken great pains with it, and have been scrupulously faithful. At the same time, I would venture to warn the reader that one perusal will be very far from making him master of it. If I may dare to say so, there is a growing feeling of something inspired and supernatural about it, as we go on studying it; and with that we cannot help experiencing, after repeated readings of it, that its novelty never seems to wear off, nor its fulness to be diminished, nor the fresh fragrance and sensible fire of its unction ever to abate. May the Holy Ghost, the Divine Zealot of Jesus and Mary, deign to give a new blessing to this work in England; and may He please to console us quickly with the canonisation of this new apostle and fiery missionary of His most dear and most immaculate Spouse; and still more with the speedy coming of that great age of the Church, which is to be the Age of Mary!

F. W. Faber
Priest of the Oratory
Presentation of our Blessed Lady, 1862

Note: See *Vie de Louis-Marie Grignion de Montfort* (Le Clerc, Paris, 1839); also the Jesuit Father Clorivière's Life of him, 1785. Grandet's Life of him (1724), as well as Bastide's memoirs of fifty missions given with the servant of God, I only know by the quotations in the Life of 1839.

Statue of St. Louis de Montfort crushing the devil, St. Peter's Basilica, Rome.

"God wishes that His holy Mother should now be more known, more loved, more honoured, than ever she has been; and this will no doubt come to pass, if the predestinate will enter, by the grace and light of the Holy Ghost, into the interior and perfect practice which I will discover to them." These words of the venerable servant of God, Louis Marie Grignion de Montfort, cannot fail to interest our piety, and to inspire us with a lively desire of learning from him so excellent a practice of honouring the most holy Virgin.

He had been drawn from his earliest infancy, in quite a particular fashion, to the love of this Queen of Angels; and in a conversation which he had with his intimate friend Monsieur Blain, two years before his death, the pious missionary confessed to him that God had favoured him with an extraordinary grace, which was the continued presence of Jesus and Mary in the bottom of his soul. This word was a mystery to Monsieur Blain; but we shall see the explanation of it in this little treatise. We shall see revealed to us there the heart of him who knew no fairer name than the slave of Jesus in Mary. We do not, however, pretend to say that this explanation will be equally understood by all. We must remember here that word of the Eternal Wisdom, "Thou hast hidden these things from the wise and prudent, and revealed them to the little ones." It has been said in the Life of the venerable servant of God, that his history will never be understood except by a Christian. It has this in common with the lives of a great number of the servants of God. We may say also that this little work will never be understood by a Christian who is too much a stranger to the maxims of humility and evangelical simplicity, and that the wise of this world will find themselves shocked at the lessons of true wisdom which they will read without penetrating their sense. *Animalis homo non percipit ea, quæ sunt Spiritus Dei. Stultitia enim est illi, et non potest intelligere, quia spiritualiter examinatur.* The man who guides himself only by natural light does not comprehend the things of the Spirit of God. They seem to him follies, because they can only be judged by a supernatural light which he has not got. But let us hasten to add, that sincere and simple souls will relish the manna hidden in the pious and touching instructions of the virtuous priest who consumed his life in evangelising the poor. They will bless Divine Providence for the treasure. They will feel themselves penetrated with love for Jesus and Mary, in reading these burning pages, which the man of God wrote in the fervour of his prayer, without ever losing sight of the presence of our Divine Saviour and His holy Mother.... In conclusion, let us say a few words on the discovery of this treatise.

At the time of the French revolution in 1793, the manuscripts which the house of the Missionaries of St. Laurent-sur-Sèvre possessed were hidden in the neighbouring farms, where they remained buried in dust for many years. Later on, those which were found were put into the library of the missionaries. But this little treatise was not at that time recognised, as was the case with some others also composed by the venerable founder of the Company. It was not till 1842 that one of the priests of the house of St. Laurent found it by chance in the library, where it had been put without being recognised, after having been mixed up with a great number of imperfect books. "After I had read a few pages," says the priest, "I took it, hoping to find it useful for making a sermon on our Lady. I read by chance the place where he speaks of his Company of Mary. I recognised the style and thoughts of our venerable founder, and his way of addressing his missionaries; and after that, I had no doubt the manuscript was his. I took it to our superior, who identified the handwriting."

[The manuscript has been examined at Rome; recognised to be the work of the venerable servant of God; most minutely examined in its doctrine; and declared to be exempt from all error which could be a bar to his canonisation.]

INTRODUCTION

I t is by the most holy Virgin Mary that Jesus has come into the world, and it is also by her that He has to reign in the world.

Mary has been singularly hidden during her life. It is on this account that the Holy Ghost and the Church call her *alma Mater,—Mother secret and hidden.* Her humility was so profound that she had no propensity on earth more powerful or more unintermitting than that of hiding herself, even from herself, as well as from every other creature, so as to be known to God only. He heard her prayers to Him, when she begged to be hidden, to be humbled, and to be treated as in all respects poor and of no account. He took pleasure in hiding her from all human creatures in her conception, in her birth, in her life, and in her resurrection and assumption. Her parents even did not know her, and the Angels often asked of each other: *Quæ est ista?* Who is that? Because the Most High either hid her from them, or if He revealed any thing of her to them, it was nothing compared to what He kept undisclosed.

God the Father consented that she should do no miracle, at least no public one, during her life, although He had given her the power. God the Son consented that she should hardly ever speak, though He had communicated His wisdom to her. God the Holy Ghost, though she was His faithful Spouse, consented that His Apostles and Evangelists should speak but very little of her, and no more than was necessary to make Jesus Christ known.

Mary is the excellent masterpiece of the Most High, of which He has reserved to Himself both the knowledge and the possession. Mary is the admirable Mother of the Son, who took pleasure in humbling and concealing her during her life, in order to favour her humility, calling her by the name of *woman* (*mulier*), as if she was a stranger, although in His heart He esteemed and loved her above all angels and all men. Mary is the sealed fountain and the faithful Spouse of the Holy Ghost, to whom He alone has entrance. Mary is the sanctuary and the repose of the Holy Trinity, where God dwells more magnificently and more divinely than in any other place in the universe, without excepting His dwelling between the Cherubim and Seraphim. Neither is it allowed to any creature, no matter how pure, to enter into that sanctuary without a great and special privilege.

I say with the Saints, The divine Mary[1] is the terrestrial Paradise of the New Adam, where He is incarnate by the operation of the Holy Ghost, in order to work there incomprehensible marvels. She is the grand and divine World of God, where there are beauties and treasures unspeakable. She is the magnificence of the Most High, where He has hidden, as in her bosom, His only Son, and in Him all that is most excellent and most precious. Oh, what grand and hidden things that mighty God has wrought in this admirable creature! How has she herself been compelled to say it, in spite of her profound humility: *Fecit mihi magna, qui potens est!*—"He that is mighty hath done great things to me." The world knows them not, because it is at once incapable and unworthy of such knowledge.

The Saints have said admirable things of this Holy City of God; and, as they themselves avow, they have never been more eloquent and more content than when they have spoken of her. Yet, after all they have said, they cry out that the height of her merits, which she has raised up to the throne of the Divinity, cannot be fully seen; that the breadth of her charity, which is broader than the earth, is in truth immeasurable; that the grandeur of her power, which she exercises even over God Himself, is incomprehensible; and finally, that the depth of her humility, and of all her virtues and graces, is an abyss which never can be sounded.

O height incomprehensible! O breadth unspeakable! O grandeur immeasurable! O abyss impenetrable! Every day, from one end of the earth to the other, in the highest heights of the heavens and in the profoundest depths of the abysses, every thing preaches, every thing publishes, the admirable Mary! The nine choirs of Angels, men of all ages, sexes, conditions, and religions, good or bad, nay even the devils themselves, willingly or unwillingly, are compelled, by the force of truth, to call her Blessed.

St. Bonaventure tells us that all the Angels in heaven cry out incessantly to her, *Sancta, sancta, sancta Maria, Dei Genitrix et Virgo,*—"Holy, holy, holy Mary, Mother of God and Virgin;" and that they offer to her millions and millions of times a day the Angelical Salutation, *Ave Maria;* prostrating themselves before her, and begging of her, in her graciousness, to honour them with some of her commands.

St. Michael, as St. Augustine says, although the prince of all the heavenly court, is the most zealous in honouring her and causing her to be honoured, while he waits always in expectation that he may have the honour to go, at her bidding, to render service to some one of her servants.

---

1. See box on next page.

The whole earth is full of her glory, especially among Christians, amongst whom she is taken as the protectress of many kingdoms, provinces, dioceses, and cities. Numbers of cathedrals are consecrated to God under her name. There is not a church without an altar in her honour, not a country or a canton where there are not some miraculous images, where all sorts of evils are cured, and all sorts of good gifts obtained. Who can count the confraternities and congregations in her honour? How many religious orders have been founded in her name and under her protection! What numbers there are of Brothers and Sisters of all these confraternities, and of religious men and women of all these orders, who publish her praises and confess her mercies! There is not a little child, who, as it lisps the Ave Maria, does not praise her. There is scarcely a sinner who, even in his obduracy, has not some spark of confidence in her. Nay the very devils in hell respect her while they fear her.

After that we must surely say with the Saints, *De Maria nunquam satis,*— "Of Mary there is never enough;" we have not yet praised, exalted, honoured, loved, and served Mary as we ought to do. She has deserved still

EDITOR'S NOTE ON DE MONTFORT'S USE OF "DIVINE MARY"

Cardinal Herbert Vaughan (1832–1903) held Saint Louis de Montfort's *True Devotion to the Blessed Virgin* in such high regard that when Bishop of Salford in Lancashire, England he had a special edition printed for all the clergy of his diocese. He personally prefaced this publication of de Montfort's Treatise with a letter addressed to the priests and religious of Salford exhorting them to take up the earnest practice of this devotion and pointing out to them the great spiritual blessings which would flow therefrom. When, upon the death of Cardinal Manning in 1892 he was appointed the third Archbishop of Westminster, he did not hesitate to do the same in his new jurisdiction for the edification of clergy in his charge. In his Preface to this 5th English edition, Cardinal Vaughan writes:

"...the word 'divine' may be used without attributing the nature of divinity to the person or thing thus qualified. We speak of our own prayers, whether addressed to God or to His saints, as a 'divine service.' The Psalmist speaks of us all as being gods and sons of the Most High; and yet no one takes offense, because the sense given to the words uttered is understood. Mary may be called 'divine' because divinely chosen for the divine office of Mother of a divine Person, Jesus Christ."

more praise, still more respect, still more love, and far more service.

After that we must say with the Holy Ghost, *Omnis gloria filiæ Regis ab intus,*—"All the glory of the King's daughter is within." It is as if all the outward glory, which heaven and earth rival each other in laying at her feet, is nothing in comparison with that which she receives within from the Creator, and which is not known by creatures, who in their littleness are unable to penetrate the secret of the secrets of the King.

After that we must cry out with the Apostle, *Nec oculus vidit, nec auris audivit, nec in cor hominis ascendit,*—"Eye has not seen, nor ear heard, nor man's heart comprehended," the beauties, the grandeurs, the excellences, of Mary,—the miracle of the miracles of grace, of nature, and of glory.

If you wish to comprehend the Mother, says a Saint, comprehend the Son; for she is the worthy Mother of God. *Hic taceat omnis lingua,*—"Here let every tongue be mute."

It is with a particular joy that my heart has dictated what I have just written, in order to show that the divine Mary has been up to this time unknown, and that this is one of the reasons that Jesus Christ is not known as He ought to be. If, then, as is certain, the kingdom of Jesus Christ is to come into the world, it will be but a necessary consequence of the knowledge of the kingdom of the most holy Virgin Mary, who brought Him into the world the first time, and will make His second advent full of splendour.

PART I

On Devotion to Our Blessed Lady in General

Miraculous fresco of Our Lady of Good Counsel, Genazzano, Italy.

CHAPTER 1

Excellence and Necessity of Devotion to Our Blessed Lady

I avow, with all the Church, that Mary, being but a mere creature that has come from the hands of the Most High, is, in comparison with His Infinite Majesty, less than an atom; or rather she is nothing at all, because He only is "He who is," and thus by consequence that grand Lord, always independent and sufficient to Himself, never had, and has not now, any absolute need of the Holy Virgin for the accomplishment of His will and for the manifestation of His glory. He has but to will, in order to do every thing. Nevertheless I say that, things being supposed as they are now, God having willed to commence and to complete His greatest works by the most holy Virgin, since He created her, we may well think He will not change His conduct in the eternal ages; for He is God, and He changes not either in His sentiments or in His conduct.

God the Father has not given His Only-begotten to the world except by Mary

Whatever sighs the patriarchs may have sent forth,—whatever prayers the prophets and the saints of the ancient law may have offered up to obtain that treasure for full four thousand years,—it was but Mary that merited it; it was but Mary who found grace before God by the force of her prayers and the eminence of her virtues. The world was unworthy, says St. Augustine, to receive the Son of God immediately from the Father's hands. He has given Him to Mary in order that the world might receive Him through her. The Son of God has made Himself Man; but it was in Mary and by Mary. God the Holy Ghost has formed Jesus Christ in Mary; but it was only after having asked her consent by one of the first ministers of His court.

God the Father has communicated to Mary His fruitfulness, as far as a mere creature was capable of it, in order that He might give her the power to produce His Son, and all the members of His mystical Body. God the Son has descended into her virginal womb, as the new Adam into the terrestrial paradise, to take His pleasure there, and to work in secret the marvels of His grace.

God made Man has found His liberty in seeing Himself imprisoned in her womb

He has made His Omnipotence shine forth in letting Himself be carried by that blessed Virgin. He has found His glory and His Father's in hiding His splendours from all creatures here below, and revealing them to Mary only. He has glorified His Independence and His Majesty, in depending on that sweet Virgin, in His Conception, in His Birth, in His Presentation in the Temple, in His Hidden Life of thirty years, and even in His Death, where she was to be present, in order that He might make with her but one same sacrifice, and be immolated to the Eternal Father by her consent; just as Isaac of old was offered by Abraham's consent to the Will of God. It is she who has suckled Him, nourished Him, supported Him, brought Him up, and then sacrificed Him for us.

O admirable and incomprehensible dependence of a God, which the Holy Ghost could not pass in silence in the Gospel, although He has hidden from us nearly all the admirable things which that Incarnate Wisdom did in His Hidden Life, as if He would enable us, by His revelation of that at least, to understand something of its price! Jesus Christ gave more glory to God the Father by submission to His Mother during those thirty years than He would have given Him in converting the whole world by the working of the most stupendous miracles. Oh, how highly we glorify God, when, to please Him, we submit ourselves to Mary, after the example of Jesus Christ, our Sole Exemplar!

If we examine narrowly the rest of our Blessed Lord's Life, we shall see that it was His Will to begin His miracles by Mary. He sanctified St. John in the womb of St. Elizabeth his mother; but it was by Mary's word. No sooner had she spoken than John was sanctified; and this was His first and greatest miracle of grace. At the marriage at Cana He changed the water into wine; but it was at Mary's humble prayer; and this was His first miracle of nature. He has begun and continued His miracles by Mary, and He will continue them to the end of ages by Mary also.

God the Holy Ghost being barren in God—that is to say, not producing another Divine Person—is become fruitful by Mary, whom He has espoused. It is with her, in her, and of her, that He has produced His Masterpiece, which is a God made Man, and whom He goes on producing in the persons of His members daily to the end of the world. The predestinate are the members of that Adorable Head. This is the reason why He, the Holy Ghost, the more He finds Mary, His dear and indissoluble Spouse, in any soul, becomes the more active and mighty in producing Jesus Christ in that soul, and that soul in Jesus Christ.

It is not that we may say that our Blessed Lady gives the Holy Ghost His fruitfulness, as if He had it not Himself. For inasmuch as He is God, He has the same fruitfulness or capacity of producing as the Father and the Son, only that He does not bring it into action, as He does not produce another Divine Person. But what we want to say is, that the Holy Ghost chose to make use of our Blessed Lady, though He had no absolute need of her, to bring His fruitfulness into action, by producing in her and by her Jesus Christ in His members; a mystery of grace unknown to even the wisest and most spiritual among Christians.

The conduct which the Three Persons of the Most Holy Trinity have deigned to pursue in the Incarnation and first coming of Jesus Christ, They still pursue daily in an invisible manner throughout the whole Church, and They will still pursue it even to the consummation of ages in the last coming of Jesus Christ.

God the Father made an assemblage of all the waters, and He named it the sea (*mare*). He has made an assemblage of all His graces, and He has called it Mary (*Maria*). This great God has a most rich treasury in which He has laid up all that He has of beauty, of splendour, of rarity, and of preciousness, even to His own Son; and this immense treasury is none other than Mary, whom the Saints have named the Treasure of the Lord, out of whose plenitude all men are made rich.

God the Son has communicated to His Mother all that He has acquired by His Life and by His Death, His infinite merits and His admirable virtues; and He has made her the treasuress of all that His Father has given Him for His inheritance. It is by her that He applies His merits to His members, and that He communicates His virtues, and distributes His graces. She is His mysterious canal; she is His aqueduct, through which He makes His mercies flow gently and abundantly.

To Mary, His faithful Spouse, God the Holy Ghost has communicated His unspeakable gifts

... and He has chosen her to be the dispensatrix of all He possesses, in such sort that she distributes to whom she wills, as much as she wills, as she wills, and when she wills, all His gifts and graces. The Holy Ghost gives no heavenly gift to men which He does not pass through her virginal hands.

Such has been the Will of God, who has willed that we should have every thing in Mary; so that she who impoverished, humbled, and hid herself even to the abyss of nothingness by her profound humility her whole life long, should now be enriched, and exalted by the Most High. Such are the sentiments of the Church and the Holy Fathers.

If I were speaking to the free-thinkers of these times, I would prove what I have said so simply, drawing it out more at length, and confirming it by the Holy Scriptures and the Fathers, quoting the original passages, and adducing various solid reasons, which may be seen at length in the book of Fr. Poiré (*La Triple Couronne de la Sainte Vierge*). But as I speak particularly to the poor and simple, who being of good-will, and having more faith than the common run of scholars, believe more simply and so more meritoriously, I content myself with putting out the truth quite simply, without stopping to quote the original passages, which they would not understand. Nevertheless, without making much research, I shall not fail from time to time to bring forward some of them. But let us now go on with our subject.

Inasmuch as grace perfects nature, and glory perfects grace, it is certain that our Lord is still, in heaven, as much the Son of Mary as He was on earth; and that, consequently, He has preserved the most perfect obedience and submission of all children towards the best of all mothers. But we must take great pains not to conceive of this dependence as any abasement or imperfection in Jesus Christ. For Mary is infinitely below her Son, who is God, and therefore she does not command Him, as a mother here below would command her child, who is below her. Mary, being altogether transformed into God by grace, and by the glory which transforms all the Saints into Him, asks nothing, wishes nothing, does nothing which is contrary to the Eternal and Immutable Will of God. When we read, then, in the writings of SS. Bernard, Bernardine, Bonaventure, and others, that in heaven and on earth every thing, even to God Himself, is subject to the Blessed Virgin, they mean to say that the authority which God has been well pleased to give her is so great, that it seems as if she has the same power as God, and that her prayers and petitions are so powerful with God, that they always pass for commandments with His Majesty, who never resists the prayer of His dear Mother, because she is always humble and conformed to His Will.

If Moses, by the force of his prayer, arrested the anger of God against the Israelites, in a manner so powerful that the Most High and infinitely merciful

Lord, being unable to resist him, told him to let Him alone, that He might be angry with and punish that rebellious people, what must we not with much greater reason think of the prayer of the humble Mary, that worthy Mother of God, which is more powerful with His Majesty than the prayers and intercessions of all the Angels and Saints both in heaven and on earth?

Mary commands in the heavens the Angels and the Blessed

As a recompense for her profound humility, God has given her the power and permission to fill with Saints the empty thrones from which the apostate angels fell by pride. Such has been the will of the Most High, who exalts the humble, that heaven, earth, and hell bend with good will or bad will to the commandments of the humble Mary, whom He has made sovereign of heaven and earth, general of His armies, treasurer of His treasures, dispenser of His graces, worker of His greatest marvels, restorer of the human race, mediatrix of men, the exterminator of the enemies of God, and the faithful companion of His grandeurs and His triumphs.

> *All the true children of God... have God for their Father, and Mary for their Mother.*

God the Father wishes to have children by Mary till the consummation of the world; and He has said to her these words, *In Jacob inhabita,*—"Dwell in Jacob,"—that is to say, Make your dwelling and residence in My predestinated children, figured by Jacob, and not in the reprobate children of the devil, figured by Esau.

Just as, in the natural and corporal generation of children, there is a father and a mother, so in the supernatural and spiritual generation there is a Father, who is God, and a Mother, who is Mary. All the true children of God, the predestinate, have God for their Father, and Mary for their Mother. He who has not Mary for his Mother, has not God for his Father. This is the reason why the reprobate, such as heretics, schismatics, and others, who hate our Blessed Lady, or regard her with contempt and indifference, have not God for their Father, however much they boast of it, simply because they have not Mary for their Mother. For if they had her for their Mother, they would love and honour her as a true and good child naturally loves and honours the mother who has given him life.

The most infallible and indubitable sign by which we may distinguish a heretic, a man of bad doctrine, a reprobate, from one of the predestinate, is that the heretic and the reprobate have nothing but contempt and indifference for our Blessed Lady, endeavouring by their words and examples to diminish the worship and love of her openly or hiddenly, and sometimes under specious pretexts. Alas! God the Father has not told Mary to dwell in them, for they are Esaus.

God the Son wishes to form Himself, and, so to speak, to incarnate Himself, every day by His dear Mother in His members

... and He has said to her, *In Israel hæreditare,*—"Take Israel for your inheritance." It is as if He had said, God the Father has given Me for an inheritance all the nations of the earth, all the men good and bad, predestinate and reprobate. The one I will lead with a rod of gold, and the others with a rod of iron. Of one I will be the Father and the Advocate, the Just Punisher of others, and the Judge of all. But as for you, My dear Mother,—you shall have for your heritage and possession only the predestinate, figured by Israel; and, as their good Mother, you shall bring them forth and maintain them; and, as their sovereign, you shall conduct them, govern and defend them.

"This man and that man is born in her," says the Holy Ghost,—*Homo et homo natus est in ea* (Ps. 86:5). According to the explanation of some of the Fathers, the first man that is born in Mary is the Man-God, Jesus Christ; the second is a mere man, the child of God and Mary by adoption. If Jesus Christ the Head of men is born in her, the predestinate who are the members of that Head ought also to be born in her by a necessary consequence. One and the same mother does not bring forth into the world the head without the members, nor the members without the head; for this would be a monster of nature. So in like manner, in the order of grace, the Head and the members are born of one and the same Mother; and if a member of the mystical Body of Jesus Christ—that is to say, one of the predestinate—was born of any other mother than Mary, who has produced the Head, he would not be one of the predestinate, nor a member of Jesus Christ, but simply a monster in the order of grace.

Besides this, Jesus being at present as much as ever the Fruit of Mary,— as heaven and earth repeat thousands and thousands of times a day, "and Blessed be the Fruit of thy womb, Jesus,"—it is certain that Jesus Christ is, for each man in particular who possesses Him, as truly the fruit of the work of Mary, as He is for the whole world in general; so that if any one of the faithful has Jesus Christ formed in his heart, he can say boldly, All thanks be to Mary! what I possess is her effect and her fruit, and without her I should never have had it. We can apply to her more truly than St. Paul applied to himself those words, *Quos iterum parturio donec formetur Christus in vobis*,—"I am in labour again with all the children of God, until Jesus Christ my Son be formed in them in the fulness of His age." St. Augustine, surpassing himself, and going beyond all I have yet said, affirms that all the predestinate, in order to be conformed to the image of the Son of God, are in this world hidden in the womb of the most holy Virgin; where they are guarded, nourished, brought up, and made to grow by that good Mother until she has brought them forth to glory after death, which is properly the day of their birth, as the Church calls the death of the just. O mystery of grace, unknown to the reprobate, and but little known even to the predestinate!

God the Holy Ghost wishes to form Himself in her, and to form elect for Himself by her

... and He has said to her, *In electis meis mitte radices*,—"Strike the roots, My Well-beloved and My Spouse, of all your virtues in My elect, in order that they may grow from virtue to virtue, and from grace to grace." I took so much complacence in you, when you lived on earth in the practice of the most sublime virtues, that I desire still to find you on earth, without your ceasing to be in heaven. For this end, reproduce yourself in My elect, that I may behold in them with complacence the roots of your invincible faith, of your profound humility, of your universal mortification, of your sublime prayer, of your ardent charity, of your firm hope, and all your virtues. You are always My Spouse, as faithful, as pure, and as fruitful as ever. Let your faith give Me My faithful, your purity My virgins, and your fertility My temples and My elect.

When Mary has struck her roots in a soul, she produces there marvels of grace, which she alone can produce, because she alone is the fruitful Virgin, who never has had, and never will have, her equal in purity and in fruitfulness.

Mary has produced, together with the Holy Ghost, the greatest thing which has been, or ever will be, which is a God-Man; and she will consequently produce the greatest things that there will be in the latter times.

The formation and education of the great Saints, who shall come at the end of the world, are reserved for her. For it is only that singular and miraculous Virgin who can produce, in union with the Holy Ghost, singular and extraordinary things.

When the Holy Ghost, her Spouse, has found Mary in a soul, He flies there. He enters there in His fulness; He communicates Himself to that soul abundantly, and to the full extent to which she makes room for her Spouse. Nay, one of the great reasons why the Holy Ghost does not now do startling wonders in our souls is because He does not find there a sufficiently great union with His faithful and indissoluble Spouse. I say indissoluble Spouse, because since that Substantial Love of the Father and the Son has espoused Mary, in order to produce Jesus Christ, the Head of the elect, and Jesus Christ in the elect, He has never repudiated her, inasmuch as she has always been fruitful and faithful. We may evidently conclude, then, from what I have said, first, that Mary has received from God a great domination over the souls of the elect; for she cannot make her residence in them, as God the Father ordered her to do, and form them in Jesus Christ, or Jesus Christ in them, and strike the roots of her virtues in their hearts, and be the indissoluble companion of the Holy Ghost in all His works of grace,—she cannot, I say, do all these things unless she has a right and domination over their souls by a singular grace of the Most High, who, having given her power over His only and Natural Son, has given it also to her over His adopted children, not only as to their bodies, which would be but little matter, but also as to their souls.

Mary is the Queen of heaven and earth by grace, as Jesus is the King of them by nature and by conquest

Now, as the kingdom of Jesus Christ consists principally in the heart and interior of a man,—according to that word, "The kingdom of God is within you,"—in like manner the kingdom of our Blessed Lady is principally in the interior of a man, that is to say, his soul; and it is principally in souls that she is more glorified with her Son than in all visible creatures, and that we can call her, as the Saints do, the Queen of hearts.

Secondly, we must conclude that, the most holy Virgin being necessary to God by a necessity which we call hypothetical, in consequence of His Will, she is far more necessary to men, in order for them to arrive at their Last End. We must not confound devotions to our Blessed Lady with devotions to the other Saints, as if devotion to her was not far more necessary than devotion to them, or as if devotion to her were a, matter of supererogation.

The learned and pious Suarez the Jesuit, the erudite and devout Justus Lipsius doctor of Louvain, and many others, have proved invincibly, in consequence of the sentiments of the Fathers (and, among others, of St. Augustine, St. Ephrem deacon of Edessa, St. Cyril of Jerusalem, St. Germanus of Constantinople, St. John Damascene, St. Anselm, St. Bernard, St. Bernardine, St. Thomas, and St. Bonaventure), that devotion to our Blessed Lady is necessary to salvation, and that, even in the opinion of Œcolampadius and some other heretics, it is an infallible mark of reprobation to have no esteem and love for the holy Virgin; while on the other hand it is an infallible mark of predestination to be entirely and truly devoted to her.

The figures and words of the Old and New Testaments prove this. The sentiments and examples of the Saints confirm it. Reason and experience teach and demonstrate it. Even the devil and his crew, constrained by the force of truth, have often been obliged to avow it in their own despite.

Among all the passages of the holy Fathers and doctors, of which I have made an ample collection, in order to prove this truth, I shall, for brevity's sake, quote but one: *Tibi devotum esse, est arma quædam salutis quæ Deus his dat, quos vult salvos fieri,*—"To be devout to you, O holy Virgin," says St. John Damascene, "is an arm of salvation which God gives to those whom He wishes to save." I could bring forward here many histories which prove the same thing, and, among others, one which is related in the chronicles of St. Dominic. There was an unhappy heretic near Carcassonne, where St. Dominic was preaching the Rosary, who was possessed by a legion of fifteen thousand devils. These evil spirits were compelled, to their confusion, by the commandment of our Blessed Lady, to avow many great and consoling truths, touching devotion to the holy Virgin; and they did this with so much force, and so much clearness, that it is not possible to read this authentic history, and the panegyric which the devil made, in spite of himself, of devotion to the most holy Mary, without shedding tears of joy, however lukewarm we may be in our devotion to her.

If devotion to the most holy Virgin Mary is necessary to all men, simply for working out their salvation, it is still more so for those who are called to any particular perfection; and I do not think any one can acquire an intimate union with our Lord, and a perfect fidelity to the Holy Ghost, without a very great union with the most holy Virgin, and a great dependence on her succour.

It is Mary alone who has found grace before God, without the aid of any other mere creature

... it is only by her that all those who have found grace before God have found it at all; and it is only by her that all those who shall come afterwards shall find it. She was full of grace when she was saluted by the Archangel Gabriel, and she was superabundantly filled with grace by the Holy Ghost when He covered her with His unspeakable Shadow; and she has so augmented, from day to day and from moment to moment, this double plenitude, that she has reached a point of grace immense and inconceivable; in such sort that the Most High has made her the sole treasurer of His treasures, and the sole dispenser of His graces, to ennoble, to exalt, and to enrich whom she wishes; to give the entry to whom she wills into the narrow way of heaven; to pass whom she wills, and in spite of all obstacles, through the strait gate of life; and to give the throne, the sceptre, and the crown of the King to whom she wills. Jesus is every where and always the Fruit and the Son of Mary; and Mary is every where the veritable tree, who bears the Fruit of life, and the true Mother, who produces it.

She was full of grace when she was saluted by the Archangel Gabriel, and she was superabundantly filled with grace by the Holy Ghost when He covered her with His unspeakable Shadow...

It is Mary alone to whom God has given the keys of the cellars of divine love, and the power to enter into the most sublime and secret ways of perfection, and the power likewise to make others enter in there also. It is Mary alone who has given to the miserable children of Eve, the faithless, the entry into the terrestrial paradise, that they may walk there agreeably with God, hide themselves there securely against their enemies, and feed themselves there deliciously, without any more fear of death, on the fruit of the trees of life and of the knowledge of good and evil, and drink in long draughts the heavenly waters of that fair fountain, which gushes forth there with abundance; or rather she is herself that terrestrial paradise, that virgin and blessed earth, from which Adam and Eve, the sinners, have been driven, and she gives no entry there except to those whom it is her pleasure to make Saints.

All the rich among the people, to make use of an expression of the Holy Ghost, according to the explanation of St. Bernard,—all the rich among the people shall supplicate thy face from age to age, and particularly at the end of the world; that is to say, the greatest Saints, the souls richest in graces and virtues, shall be the most assiduous in praying to our Blessed Lady, and in having her always present as their perfect model to imitate, and their powerful aid to give them succour.

I have said that this would come to pass particularly at the end of the world, and indeed presently, because the Most High with His holy Mother has to form for Himself great Saints, who shall surpass most of the other Saints in sanctity, as much as the cedars of Lebanon outgrow the little shrubs, as has been revealed to a holy soul, whose life has been written by a great servant of God.

These great souls, full of grace and zeal, shall be chosen to match themselves against the enemies of God, who shall rage on all sides; and they shall be singularly devout to our Blessed Lady, illuminated by her light, nourished by her milk, led by her spirit, supported by her arm, and sheltered under her protection, so that they shall fight with one hand and build with the other. With one hand they shall fight, overthrow, and crush the heretics with their heresies, the schismatics with their schisms, the idolaters with their idolatries, and the sinners with their impieties. With the other hand they shall build the temple of the true Solomon, and the mystical city of God; that is to say, the most holy Virgin, called by the holy Fathers the temple of Solomon and the city of God. By their words and their examples they shall bend the whole world to true devotion to Mary. This shall bring upon them many enemies; but it shall also bring many victories and much glory for God alone. It is this which God revealed to St. Vincent Ferrer, the great apostle of his age, as he has sufficiently noted in one of his works.

It is this which the Holy Ghost seems to have prophesied in the fifty-eighth Psalm, of which these are the words: *Et scient quia Dominus dominabitur Jacob, et finium terræ; convertentur ad vesperam, et famem patientur ut canes, et circuibunt civitatem,*—"And they shall know that God will rule Jacob, and all the ends of the earth; they shall return at evening, and shall suffer hunger like dogs, and shall go round about the city."

This city which men shall find at the end of the world to convert themselves in, and to satisfy the hunger they have for justice, is the most holy Virgin, who is called by the Holy Ghost the City of God.

It is by Mary that the salvation of the world has begun, and it is by Mary that it must be consummated

Mary has hardly appeared at all in the first coming of Jesus Christ, in order that men, as yet but little instructed and enlightened on the Person of her Son, should not remove themselves from Him, in attaching themselves too strongly and too grossly to her. This would have apparently taken place, if she had been known, because of the admirable charms which the Most High had bestowed even upon her exterior. This is so true that St. Denys the Areopagite has informed us in his writings that when he saw our Blessed Lady, he should have taken her for a Divinity, in consequence of her secret charms and incomparable beauty, had not the Faith in which he was well established taught him the contrary. But in the second coming of Jesus Christ, Mary has to be made known and revealed by the Holy Ghost, in order that by her Jesus Christ may be known, loved, and served. The reasons which moved the Holy Ghost to hide His Spouse during her life, and to reveal her but very little since the preaching of the Gospel, subsist no longer.

God, then, wishes to reveal and discover Mary, the masterpiece of His hands, in these latter times:

- Because she hid herself in this world, and put herself lower than the dust by her profound humility, having obtained of God and of His Apostles and Evangelists that she should not be made manifest.

- Because, being the masterpiece of the hands of God, as well here below by grace as in heaven by glory, He wishes to be glorified and praised in her by those who are living upon the earth.

- As she is the aurora which precedes and discovers the Sun of Justice, who is Jesus Christ, she ought to be recognised and perceived, in order that Jesus Christ may be so.

- Being the way by which Jesus Christ came to us the first time, she will also be the way by which He will come the second time, though not in the same manner.

- Being the sure means and the straight and immaculate way to go to Jesus Christ, and to find Him perfectly, it is by her that the holy souls, who are to shine forth especially in sanctity, have to find our Lord. He who shall find Mary shall find life;

that is, Jesus Christ, who is the Way, the Truth, and the Life. But no one can find Mary who does not seek her; and no one can seek her, who does not know her: for we cannot seek or desire an unknown object. It is necessary, then, for the greater knowledge and glory of the Most Holy Trinity, that Mary should be more known than ever.

- Mary must shine forth more than ever in mercy, in might, and in grace, in these latter times: in mercy, to bring back and lovingly receive the poor strayed sinners who shall be converted and shall return to the Catholic Church; in might, against the enemies of God, idolaters, schismatics, Mahometans, Jews, and souls hardened in impiety, who shall rise in terrible revolt against God to seduce all those who shall be contrary to them, and to make them fall by promises and threats; and, finally, she must shine forth in grace, in order to animate and sustain the valiant soldiers and faithful servants of Jesus Christ, who shall do battle for His interests.

- And, lastly, Mary must be terrible to the devil and his crew, as an army ranged in battle, principally in these latter times, because the devil, knowing that he has but little time, and now less than ever, to destroy souls, will every day redouble his efforts and his combats. He will presently raise up new persecutions, and will put terrible snares before the faithful servants and true children of Mary, whom it gives him more trouble to surmount than it does to conquer others.

It is principally of these last and cruel persecutions of the devil, which shall go on increasing daily till the reign of Antichrist, that we ought to understand that first and celebrated prediction and curse of God, pronounced in the terrestrial Paradise against the serpent. It is to our purpose to explain this here, for the glory of the most holy Virgin, for the salvation of her children, and for the confusion of the devil.

Inimicitias ponam inter te et mulierem, et semen tuum et semen illius; ipsa conteret caput tuum, et tu insidiaberis calcaneo ejus (Gen. 3:15),—"I will put enmities between thee and the woman, and thy seed and her seed; she shall crush thy head, and thou shalt lie in wait for her heel."

God has never made or formed but one enmity
...but it is an irreconcilable one, which shall endure and develop even to

the end. It is between Mary, His worthy Mother, and the devil,—between the children and the servants of the Blessed Virgin and the children and instruments of Lucifer. The most terrible of all the enemies which God has set up against the devil is His holy Mother, Mary. He has inspired her, even since the days of the earthly Paradise, though she existed then only in His idea, with so much hatred against that cursed enemy of God, with so much industry in unveiling the malice of that old serpent, with so much power to conquer, to overthrow, and to crush that proud impious rebel, that he fears her not only more than all Angels and men, but in some sense more than God Himself. It is not that the anger, the hatred, and the power of God are not infinitely greater than those of the Blessed Virgin, for the perfections of Mary are limited, but it is, first, because Satan, being proud, suffers infinitely more from being beaten and punished by a little and humble handmaid of God, and her humility humbles him more than the Divine power; and, secondly, because God has given Mary such a great power against the devils, that, as they have often been obliged to confess, in spite of themselves, by the mouths of the possessed, they fear one of her sighs for a soul more than the prayers of all the Saints, and one of her menaces against them more than all other torments.

> *God has not only set an enmity but* enmities, *not simply between Mary and the devil, but between the race of the holy Virgin and the race of the devil...*

What Lucifer has lost by pride, Mary has gained by humility. What Eve has damned and lost by disobedience, Mary has saved by obedience. Eve, in obeying the serpent, has destroyed all her children together with herself, and has delivered them to him; Mary, being perfectly faithful to God, has saved all her children and servants together with herself, and has consecrated them to His Majesty.

God has not only set an enmity but *enmities*, not simply between Mary and the devil, but between the race of the holy Virgin and the race of the devil; that is to say, God has set enmities, antipathies, and secret hatreds between the true children and the servants of Mary, and the children and servants of the devil. They do not love each other mutually. They have no inward correspondence with each other. The children of Belial, the slaves of Satan, the friends of the world (for it is the same thing), have always up to this time persecuted those who belong to our Blessed Lady, and will in future persecute them more than ever; just as of old Cain persecuted his brother Abel, and Esau his brother Jacob, who are the figures of the reprobate and the predestinate. But the humble Mary will always have the victory over that proud spirit, and so great a victory that she will go the length of crushing his head, where his pride dwells. She will always discover the malice of the serpent. She will always counterwork his infernal mines and dissipate his diabolical counsels, and will guarantee even to the end of time her faithful servants from his cruel claw. But the power of Mary over all the devils will especially break out in the latter times, when Satan will lay his snares against her heel; that is to say, her humble slaves and her poor children, whom she will raise up to make war against him. They shall be little and poor in the world's esteem, and abased before all, like the heel, trodden underfoot and persecuted as the heel is by the other members of the body. But in return for this, they shall be rich in the grace of God, which Mary shall distribute to them abundantly. They shall be great and exalted before God in sanctity, superior to all other creatures by their animated zeal, and leaning so strongly on the divine succour, that, with the humility of their heel, in union with Mary, they shall crush the head of the devil, and cause Jesus Christ to triumph.

In a word, God wishes that His holy Mother should be at present more known, more loved, more honoured, than she has ever been

This no doubt will take place, if the predestinate enter, with the grace and light of the Holy Ghost, into the interior and perfect practice which I will disclose to them shortly. Then they will see clearly, as far as faith allows, that beautiful Star of the Sea. They will arrive happily in harbour, following its guidance, in spite of the tempests and the pirates. They will know the grandeurs of that Queen, and will consecrate themselves entirely to her service, as subjects and slaves of love. They will experience her sweetnesses and her maternal goodnesses, and they will love her tenderly like well-beloved children. They will know the mercies of which she is full, and the need they have of her succour; and they will have recourse to her in all things, as to their dear advocate and mediatrix with Jesus Christ. They will know what is the most sure, the most easy, the most short, and the most

perfect means by which to go to Jesus Christ; and they will deliver themselves to Mary, body and soul, without reserve, that they may thus be all
for Jesus Christ.

But who shall be those servants, slaves, and children of Mary?

They shall be a burning fire of the ministers of the Lord, who shall kindle
the fire of divine love every where, and *sicut sagittæ in manu potentis*,—
"like sharp arrows in the hand of the powerful" Mary to pierce her enemies.
They shall be the sons of Levi, well purified by the fire of great tribulation,
and closely adhering to God; who shall carry the gold of love in their heart,
the incense of prayer in their spirit, and the myrrh of mortification in their
body; and they shall be every where the good odour of Jesus Christ to the
poor and to the little, while they shall be an odour of death to the great, to
the rich, and to the proud worldlings.

They shall be clouds thundering and flying through the air at the least
breath of the Holy Ghost; who, without attaching themselves to any thing,
without being astonished at any thing, without putting themselves in pain
about any thing, shall shower forth the rain of the Word of God and of life
eternal. They shall thunder against sin; they shall storm against the world;
they shall strike the devil and his crew; and they shall strike further and
further, for life or for death, with their two-edged sword of the Word of
God, all those to whom they shall be sent on the part of the Most High.

They shall be the true apostles of the latter times

...to whom the Lord of Hosts shall give the word and the might to work
marvels, and to carry off the glory of the spoils of His enemies. They shall
sleep without gold or silver, and, what is more, without care, in the middle
of the other priests, ecclesiastics, and clerks, *inter medios cleros*; and yet
they shall have the silvered wings of the dove, to go, with the pure intention
of the glory of God and the salvation of souls, wheresoever the Holy Ghost
shall call them. Neither shall they leave behind them, in the places where
they have preached, any thing but the gold of charity, which is the accomplishment of the whole law. In a word, we know that they shall be true disciples of Jesus Christ, who, marching in the footsteps of His poverty,
humility, contempt of the world, and charity, shall teach the strait way of
God in the pure truth, according to the holy Gospel, and not according to
the maxims of the world, without putting themselves in pain about things,

or accepting persons, without sparing, fearing, or listening to any mortal, however influential he may be.

They shall have in their mouths the two-edged sword of the Word of God. They shall carry on their shoulders the bloody standard of the cross, the crucifix in their right hand and the rosary in their left, the sacred names of Jesus and Mary on their hearts, and the modesty and mortification of Jesus Christ in their own behaviour. These are the great men who shall come. But Mary shall be there by the order of the Most High, to extend His empire over that of the impious, the idolaters, and the Mahometans. But when and how shall this be? God alone knows. It is for us to hold our tongues, to pray, to sigh, and to wait: *exspectans exspectavi*,—"expecting I have expected."

Painting of Our Lady of the Blessed Sacrament, Chiesa dei Santi Claudio e Andrea dei Borgognoni, Rome.

CHAPTER 2

True Devotion to Our Blessed Lady: Fundamental Truths

Having said something so far of the necessity which we have of the devotion to the most holy Virgin, I must now show in what this devotion consists. This I will do, by God's help, after I shall have first presupposed some fundamental truths, which shall throw light on that grand and solid devotion which I desire to disclose.

First Truth

Jesus Christ our Saviour, true God and true Man, ought to be the last end of all our other devotions, else they are false and delusive. Jesus Christ is the *alpha* and *omega*, the beginning and the end of all things. We labour not, as the Apostle says, except to render every man perfect in Jesus Christ; because it is in Him alone that the whole plenitude of the Divinity dwells, together with all the other plenitudes of graces, virtues, and perfections; because it is in Him alone that we have been blessed with all spiritual benediction; and because He is our only Master, who has to teach us; our only Lord, on whom we ought to depend; our only Head, to whom we must belong; our only Model, to whom we should conform ourselves; our only Physician, who can heal us; our only Shepherd, who can feed us; our only Way, who can lead us; our only Truth, who can make us grow; our only Life, who can animate us; and our only All in all things, who can suffice us. There has been no other name given under heaven, except the name of Jesus, by which we can be saved. God has laid no other foundation of our salvation, of our perfection, and of our glory, except Jesus Christ. Every building which is not built upon that firm rock is founded upon the moving sand, and sooner or later will fall infallibly. Every one of the faithful who is not united to Him, as a branch to the stock of the vine, shall fall, shall wither, and shall be fit only to be cast into the fire. If we are in Jesus Christ and Jesus Christ in us, we have no condemnation to fear. Neither the Angels of heaven, nor the men of earth, nor the devils of hell, nor any other creatures, can injure us; because they cannot separate us from the love of God which is in Jesus Christ. By Jesus Christ, with Jesus Christ, in Jesus Christ, we can do all things; we can render all honour and glory to the Father in the unity of the Holy Ghost; we can become perfect ourselves, and be to our neighbour a good odour of eternal life.

If, then, we establish the solid devotion to our Blessed Lady, it is only to establish more perfectly the devotion to Jesus Christ

...and to put forward an easy and secure means for finding Jesus Christ. If devotion to our Lady removed us from Jesus Christ, we should have to reject it as an illusion of the devil; but on the contrary, so far from this being the case, there is nothing which makes devotion to our Lady more necessary for us, as I have already shown, and will show still further hereafter, than that it is the means of finding Jesus Christ perfectly, of loving Him tenderly, and of serving Him faithfully.

I here turn for one moment to Thee, O my sweet Jesus, to complain lovingly to Thy Divine Majesty that the greater part of Christians, even the most learned, do not know the necessary union which there is between Thee and Thy holy Mother. Thou, Lord, art always with Mary, and Mary is always with Thee, and she cannot be without Thee, else she would cease to be what she is. She is so transformed into Thee by grace that she lives no more, that she is as though she were not. It is Thou only, my Jesus, who livest and reignest in her more perfectly than in all the Angels and the Blessed. Ah! if we knew the glory and the love which Thou receivest in this admirable creature, we should have very different thoughts both of Thee and her from what we have now. She is so intimately united with Thee, that it were easier to separate the light from the sun, the heat from the fire. I say more: it were easier to separate from Thee all the Angels and the Saints than the divine Mary, because she loves Thee more ardently, and glorifies Thee more perfectly, than all other creatures put together.

After that, my sweet Master, is it not an astonishingly pitiable thing to see the ignorance and the darkness of all men here below in regard to Thy holy Mother? I speak not so much of idolaters and pagans, who, knowing Thee not, care not to know Thee; I speak not even of heretics and schismatics, who care not to be devout to Thy holy Mother, being separated as they are from Thee and Thy holy Church: but I speak of Catholic Christians, and even of doctors amongst Catholics, who make profession of teaching truths to others, and yet know not Thee nor Thy holy Mother, except in a speculative, dry, barren, and indifferent manner. These doctors speak but rarely of thy holy Mother, and of the devotion which we ought to have to her, because they fear, so they say, lest we should abuse it, and should do some injury to Thee in too much honouring Thy holy Mother. If they see or hear any one devout to our Blessed Lady, speaking often of his devotion to that good Mother in a tender, strong, and persuasive way, as of a secure means without delusion, as of a short road without danger, as of an immaculate way without imperfection, and as of a wonderful secret for finding and loving Thee perfectly, they cry out against him, and give him a thousand false reasons by way of proving to him that he ought not to talk so much of our Blessed Lady, that there are great abuses in that devotion, and that we must direct our energies to destroy these abuses, and to speak of Thee, rather than to incline the people to devotion to our Blessed Lady, whom they already love sufficiently.

O my sweet Jesus... Does devotion to Thy holy Mother hinder devotion to Thyself? Is it that she attributes to herself the honour which we pay her?

We hear them sometimes speak of devotion to Thy holy Mother, not for the purpose of establishing it and persuading men to it, but to destroy the abuses which are made of it, while all the time these teachers are without piety or tender devotion towards Thyself, simply because they have none for Mary. They regard the Rosary, the Scapular, and the Chaplet as devotions proper for weak and ignorant minds, and without which men can save themselves; and if there falls into their hands any poor client of our Lady, who says his Rosary, or has any other practice of devotion towards her, they soon change his spirit and his heart. Instead of the Rosary, they counsel him the seven Penitential Psalms. Instead of devotion to the holy Virgin, they counsel him devotion to Jesus Christ.

O my sweet Jesus, have these people got Thy spirit? Do they please Thee in acting thus? Is it to please Thee, to spare one single effort to please Thy Mother for fear of thereby displeasing Thee? Does devotion to Thy holy Mother hinder devotion to Thyself? Is it that she attributes to herself the honour which we pay her? Is it that she makes a side for herself apart? Is it that she is an alien, who has no union with Thee? Does it displease Thee that we should try to please her? Is it to separate or to alienate ourselves from Thy love to give ourselves to her and to love her? Yet, my sweet Master, the greater part of the learned could not shrink more from devotion to Thy holy Mother, and could not show more indifference to it, if all that I have just said were true! Keep me, Lord,—keep me from their sentiments and their practices, and give me some share in the sentiments of gratitude, esteem, respect, and love which Thou hadst in regard to Thy holy Mother, in order that I may love Thee and glorify Thee all the more by imitating and following Thee more closely.

So, as if up to this point I had still said nothing in honour of Thy holy Mother, "give me now the grace to praise her worthily,"—*fac me digne tuam Matrem collaudare,*—in spite of all her enemies, who are Thine as well; and grant me to say loudly with the Saints, *Non præsumat aliquis Deum se habere propitium, qui benedictam Matrem offensam habuerit,*—"Let not that man presume to look for the mercy of God who offends His holy Mother." To obtain of Thy mercy a true devotion to Thy holy Mother, and to inspire it to the whole earth, make me to love Thee ardently; and for that end receive the burning prayer which I make to Thee with St. Augustine and thy true friends:

> "Tu es Christus, pater meus sanctus, Deus meus pius, rex meus magnus, pastor meus bonus, magister meus unus, adjutor meus optimus, dilectus meus pulcherrimus, panis meus vivus, sacerdos meus in æternum, dux meus ad patriam, lux mea vera, dulcedo mea sancta, via mea recta, sapientia mea præclara, simplicitas mea pura, concordia mea pacifica, custodia mea tota, portio mea bona, salus mea sempiterna.

> "Christe Jesu, amabilis Domine, cur amavi, quare concupivi in omni vitâ meâ, quidquam præter te Jesum Deum meum? Ubi eram quando tecum mente non eram? Jam ex hoc nunc, omnia desideria mea, incalescite et effluite in Dominum Jesum; currite, satis hactenus tardâstis; properate, quò pergitis; quærite quam quæritis. Jesu, qui non amat te, anathema sit; qui te non amat, amaritudinibus repleatur.

> "O dulcis Jesu, te amet, in te delectetur, te admiretur omnis sensus bonus tuæ conveniens laudi; Deus cordis mei et pars mea, Christe Jesu, deficiat cor meum spiritu suo, et vivas tu in me, et

> concalescat spiritu meo vivus carbo amoris tui, et excrescat in ignem perfectum, ardeat jugiter in arâ cordis mei, ferveat in medullis meis, flagret in absconditis animæ meæ; in die consummationis meæ consummatus inveniar apud te." ***Amen.***

I have desired to put in Latin this admirable prayer of St. Augustine, in order that those who understand Latin may say it every day, to ask for the love of Jesus, which we seek by the divine Mary.

[The translator thinks it well to give the prayer in English, and without throwing it into the small print of a note.]

PRAYER OF SAINT AUGUSTINE

Thou art Christ, my holy Father, my tender God, my great King, my good Shepherd, my one Master, my best Helper, my most Beautiful and my Beloved, my living Bread, my Priest for ever, my Leader to my country, my true Light, my holy Sweetness, my straight Way, my excellent Wisdom, my pure Simplicity, my pacific Harmony, my whole Guard, my good Portion, my everlasting Salvation.

Christ Jesus, sweet Lord, why have I ever loved, why in my whole life have I ever desired, any thing except Thee, Jesus my God? Where was I, when I was not in Thy mind with Thee? Now, from this time forth, do ye, all my desires, grow hot, and flow out upon the Lord Jesus; run,—ye have been tardy so far; hasten whither ye are going; seek whom ye are seeking. O Jesus, may he who loves Thee not be anathema; may he who loves Thee not be filled with bitterness!

O sweet Jesus, may every good feeling that is fitted for Thy praise love Thee, delight in Thee, admire Thee, God of my heart, and my Portion! Christ Jesus, may my heart faint away in spirit, and mayest Thou be my life within me! May the live coal of Thy love grow hot within my spirit, and break forth into a perfect fire; may it burn incessantly on the altar of my heart; may it glow in my innermost being; may it blaze in hidden recesses of my soul; and in the day of my consummation may I be found consummated with Thee! ***Amen.***

Second Truth

We must conclude, from what Jesus Christ is with regard to us, that we do not belong to ourselves, but, as the Apostle says, are entirely His, as His members and His slaves, whom He has bought at an infinitely dear price,—the price of all His Blood. Before Baptism we belonged to the devil, as his slaves; but Baptism has made us true slaves of Jesus Christ, who have no right to live, to work, or to die, except to bring forth fruit for that God-Man, to glorify Him in our bodies, and to let Him reign in our souls, because we are His conquest, His acquired people, and His inheritance. It is for the same reason that the Holy Ghost compares us, **1.** to trees planted along the waters of grace in the field of the Church, who ought to bring forth their fruit in their seasons; **2.** to the branches of a vine, of which Jesus Christ is the stock, and which must yield good grapes; **3.** to a flock of which Jesus Christ is the shepherd, and which is to multiply and give milk; **4.** to a good land, of which God is the labourer, in which the seed multiplies itself, and brings forth thirty-fold, sixty-fold, and a hundred-fold. Jesus Christ cursed the unfruitful fig-tree, and gave sentence against the useless servant, who had not made any profit on his talent. All this proves to us that Jesus Christ wishes to receive some fruits from our wretched selves, namely, our good works, because those good works belong to Him alone: *Creati in operibus bonis in Christo Jesu,*—"Created in good works in Christ Jesus,"—which words show both that Jesus Christ is the sole principle, and ought to be the sole end of all our good works, and also that we ought to serve Him, not as servants on wages, but as slaves of love. I will explain myself:

Here on earth there are two ways of belonging to another, and of depending on his authority, namely, simple service and slavery,—what we mean by a servant, and what we mean by a slave.

By common service amongst Christians a man engages himself to serve another, during a certain time, at a certain rate of wages or of recompense.

By slavery a man is entirely dependent on another for his whole life, and must serve his master without pretending to any wages or reward, just as one of his beasts, over which he has the right of life and death.

There are three sorts of slavery: a slavery of nature, a slavery of constraint, and a slavery of the will. All creatures are slaves of God in the first sense: *Domini est terra et plenitudo ejus,*—"The earth is the Lord's, and the fulness of it." The demons and the damned are slaves in the second sense; the just and the Saints in the third. The slavery of the will is the most glorious to God, who looks at the heart, claims the heart, and calls Himself the God of the heart; that is, of the loving will, because by that slavery we make choice of God and His service above all things, even when nature does not oblige us to it.

There is an entire difference between a servant and a slave:

1. A servant does not give all he is, all he has, and all he can acquire by himself or by another, to his master; but the slave gives himself whole and entire to his master, all he has and all he can gain, without any exception.

2. The servant exacts wages for the services which he performs for his master; but the slave can exact nothing, whatever assiduity, whatever industry, whatever energy, he may have at his work.

3. The servant can leave his master when he pleases, or at least when the time of his service shall be expired; but the slave has no right to quit his master at his will.

4. The master of the servant has no right of life and death over him, so that if he kill him like one of his beasts of burden, he would commit an unjust homicide; but the master of the slave has by the law a right of life and death over him, so that he may sell him to any body he likes, or kill him, as if he stood on the same level as one of his horses.

5. Lastly, the servant is only for a time in his master's service; the slave is for always.

There is nothing among men which makes us belong to another more than slavery. There is nothing among Christians which makes us more absolutely belong to Jesus Christ and His holy Mother than the slavery of the will, according to the example of Jesus Christ Himself, who took on Him the form of a slave for love of us,—*Forman servi accipiens,*—and also according to the example of the holy Virgin, who is called the servant and the slave of the Lord. The Apostle calls himself, as by a title of honour, *Servus Christi,*—"The slave of Christ." Christians are often called in the Holy Scriptures *Servi Christi,* "Slaves of Christ,"—which word *servus,* as a great man has truly remarked, signified in old times nothing but a slave, because there were no servants then like those of the present day. Masters were served only either by slaves or by freedmen. It is this which the catechism of the Holy Council of Trent, in order to leave no doubt about our being slaves of Jesus Christ, expresses by an unequivocal term, in calling us *Mancipia Christi,*—"Slaves of Jesus Christ."

Having premised this, I say that we ought to be to Jesus Christ and to serve Him not only as mercenary servants, but as loving slaves, who, by an effect of great love, give themselves up to serve Him in the quality of slaves, for the simple honour of belonging to Him. Before Baptism we were the slaves of the devil; Baptism has made us the slaves of Jesus Christ: Christians must needs be either the slaves of the devil or the slaves of Jesus Christ.

What I say absolutely of Jesus Christ, I say relatively of our Blessed Lady. Jesus Christ, having chosen her for the inseparable companion of His life, of His death, of His glory, and of His power in heaven and upon earth, has given her by grace, relatively to His Majesty, all the same rights and privileges which He possesses by nature. *Quidquid Deo convenit per naturam, Mariæ convenit per gratiam,*—"All that is fitting to God by nature is fitting to Mary by grace,"—say the Saints; so that, according to them, Mary and Jesus having but the same will and the same power, the two have the same subjects, servants, and slaves.

> *Our Blessed Lady is the means our Lord made use of to come to us. She is also the means which we must make use of to go to Him.*

We may, therefore, following the sentiments of the Saints and of many great men, call ourselves, and make ourselves, the loving slaves of the most holy Virgin, in order to be by that very means the more perfectly the slaves of Jesus Christ. Our Blessed Lady is the means our Lord made use of to come to us. She is also the means which we must make use of to go to Him. For she is not like all the rest of creatures, who, if we should attach ourselves to them, might rather draw us away from God than draw us near Him. The strongest inclination of Mary is to unite us to Jesus Christ her Son; and the strongest inclination of the Son is, that we should come to Him by His holy Mother. It is to honour and please Him, just as it would be to do honour and pleasure to a king, to become more perfectly his subject and his slave, by making ourselves the slaves of the queen. It is on this account that the holy Fathers, and St. Bonaventure after them, said that our Lady was the way to go to our Lord: *Via veniendi ad Christum est appropinquare ad illam,*—"The way of coming to Christ is to draw near to her."

Moreover, if, as I have said, the holy Virgin is the Queen and Sovereign of heaven and of earth, then is it not true what has been said by St. Anselm,

St. Bernard, St. Bernardine, and St. Bonaventure,—has she not as many subjects and slaves as there are creatures? *Imperio Dei omnia subjiciuntur, et Virgo; ecce imperio Virginis omnia subjiciuntur, et Deus*,—"All things, the Virgin included, are subject to the empire of God; behold all things, and God included, are subject to the empire of the Virgin." Is it not reasonable that amongst so many slaves of constraint, there should be some of love, who of their own good will, in the quality of slaves, should choose Mary for their mistress? What! are men and devils to have their voluntary slaves, and Mary to have none? What! shall a king hold it to be for his honour that the queen, his companion, should have slaves over whom she has the right of life and death, because the honour and power of the one is the honour and power of the other, and yet are we to think that our Lord, who, as the best of all Sons, has divided His entire power with His holy Mother, shall take it ill that she too has her slaves? Has He less respect and love for His Mother than Ahasuerus had for Esther, or than Solomon for Bathsebee? Who shall dare to say so, or even to think it?

But whither is my pen hurrying me? Why am I stopping here to prove a thing so plain? If we do not wish to call ourselves slaves of the Blessed Virgin, what matter? Let us make ourselves and call ourselves slaves of Jesus Christ; for that is to be the slave of the holy Virgin, inasmuch as Jesus is the fruit and the glory of Mary; and it is this very thing which we do, by the devotion of which we are hereafter to speak.

Third Truth

Our best actions are ordinarily stained and corrupted by the ground of evil which is so deeply laid up in us. When we put clean and clear water into a vessel which has a foul and evil smell, or wine into a cask the inside of which has been spoilt by another wine which has been in it, the clear water and the good wine are spoilt, and readily take the bad odour. In like manner, when God puts into the vessel of our soul, spoilt by original and actual sin, His graces and heavenly dews, or the delicious wine of His love, His gifts are ordinarily spoilt and corrupted by the bad leaven and the evil which sin has left within us. Our actions, even the most sublime and virtuous, feel the effects of it. It is therefore of great importance in the acquiring of perfection, which it must be remembered is only acquired by union with Jesus Christ, to empty ourselves of every thing which is bad within us; otherwise our Lord, who is infinitely pure and hates infinitely the least stain upon our souls, will cast us out from His presence, and will not unite Himself to us.

To empty ourselves of ourselves, we must, first, thoroughly recognise, by the light of the Holy Ghost, our inward corruption, our incapacity for every good thing useful for salvation, our weakness in all things, our inconstancy at all times, our indignity of every grace, and our iniquity in every position. The sin of our first father has spoilt us all, soured us, puffed us up and corrupted us, as the leaven sours, puffs, and corrupts the paste into which it is put. The actual sins which we have committed, whether mortal or venial, pardoned though they may be, have nevertheless increased our concupiscence, our weakness, our inconstancy, and our corruption, and have left evil consequences in our souls. Our bodies are so corrupted that they are called by the Holy Ghost bodies of sin, conceived in sin, nourished in sin, and capable of all sin,—bodies subject to thousands of maladies, which go on corrupting from day to day, and which engender nothing but disease, vermin, and corruption.

Our soul, united to our body, has become so carnal, that it is called flesh. "All flesh having corrupted its way," we have nothing for our portion but pride and blindness in the spirit, hardness in the heart, weakness and inconstancy in the soul, concupiscence, revolted passions, and sicknesses in the body. We are naturally prouder than peacocks, more grovelling on the earth than toads, more vile than unclean animals, more envious than serpents, more gluttonous than hogs, more furious than tigers, lazier than tortoises, weaker than reeds, and more capricious than weathercocks. We have down in our own selves nothing but nothingness and sin, and we deserve nothing but the anger of God, and the everlasting hell.

After this, ought we to be astonished if our Lord has said, that whosoever wishes to follow Him must renounce himself and hate his own soul, and that whosoever shall love his own soul shall lose it, and whosoever shall hate it shall save it? He who is infinite Wisdom does not give commandments without reason, and He has only commanded us to hate ourselves, because we so richly deserve to be hated. Nothing is worthier of love than God, and nothing is worthier of hatred than ourselves.

Secondly, in order to empty ourselves of ourselves, we must die to ourselves daily. That is to say, we must renounce the operations of the powers of our soul, and of the senses of our body. We must see as if we saw not, understand as if we understood not, and make use of the things of this world as if we made no use of them at all. This is what St. Paul calls dying daily,—*Quotidie morior.* "If the grain of corn falling on the earth does not die, it remains earth, and brings forth no good fruit,"—*Nisi granum frumenti, cadens in terram, mortuum fuerit, ipsum solum manet.* If we die not to ourselves, and if our holiest devotions do not incline us to this necessary and useful death, we shall bring forth no fruit worth any thing, and our devotions will become useless. All our justices will be stained by self-love and our own will; and this will cause God to hold in abomination the greatest sacrifices we can make, and the best actions we can do; so that at our death we shall find our hands empty of virtues and of merits, and we shall not have one spark of pure love, which is only communicated to souls dead to themselves, souls whose life is hidden with Jesus Christ in God.

We must choose, therefore, among all the devotions to the Blessed Virgin, the one which draws us most towards this death to ourselves, inasmuch as it will be the best and the most sanctifying. For we must not think that all that shines is gold, that all that tastes sweet is honey, or all that is easy to do and is done by the greatest number is sanctifying. As there are secrets of nature to do in a short time, at little cost and with facility, natural operations, so also in like manner there are secrets in the order of grace to do in a short time, with sweetness and facility, supernatural operations, such as emptying ourselves of self, filling ourselves with God, and becoming perfect.

The practice which I am about to disclose is one of these secrets of grace, unknown by the greater number of Christians, known even to few of the devout, and practised and relished by a far less number still. But in order to begin to disclose this practice, let us consider a fourth truth, which is a consequence of the third.

Fourth Truth

It is more perfect, because it is more humble, not to approach God of ourselves, without taking a mediator. The very foundation of our nature, as I have just shown, is so corrupted, that if we lean on our own works, industries, and preparations, in order to reach God and to please Him, it is certain that our justices will be defiled, or be of little weight before God, to engage Him to unite Himself to us, and to hear us. It is not without reason that God has given us mediators with His Majesty. He has seen our unworthiness and incapacity. He has had pity upon us; and, in order to give us access to His mercies, He has provided us with powerful intercessors with His grandeur, insomuch that to neglect these mediators, and to draw near to His holiness directly, and without any recommendation, is to fail in humility. It is to fail in respect towards God, so high and so holy. It is to make less account of that King of kings than we should make of a king or prince of earth, whom we should not willingly approach without some friend to speak for us.

Our Lord is our Advocate and Mediator of redemption with God the Father. It is by Him that we ought to pray, in union with the whole Church triumphant and militant. It is by Him that we have access to the Majesty of the Father, before whom we ought never to appear except leaning on the merits, and indeed clothed with the merits, of His Son; just as the young Jacob came before his father Isaac in the skins of the kids to receive his benediction.

But have we not need of a mediator with the Mediator Himself? Is our purity great enough to unite us directly to Him, and by ourselves? Is He not God, in all things equal to His Father, and by consequence the Holy of Holies, as worthy of respect as His Father? If, by His infinite charity, He has made Himself our bail and our Mediator with God His Father, in order to appease Him and to pay Him what we owed Him, are we on that account to have less respect and less fear for His Majesty and His Sanctity?

MARY – OUR MEDIATOR WITH THE MEDIATOR HIMSELF

Let us say boldly with St. Bernard, that we have need of a mediator with the Mediator Himself, and that it is the divine Mary who is the most capable of filling that charitable office. It is by her that Jesus Christ came, and it is by her that we must go to Him. If we fear to go directly to Jesus Christ our God, whether because of His infinite greatness, or because of our vileness, or because of our sins, let us boldly implore the aid and intercession of Mary our Mother. She is good, she is tender, she has nothing in her austere or repulsive, nothing too sublime and too brilliant. In seeing her, we see our pure nature. She is not the sun, who, by the vivacity of his rays, blinds us because of our weakness; but she is fair and gentle as the moon, which receives the light of the sun, and tempers it to render it more suitable to our capacity. She is so charitable that she repels none of those who ask her intercession, no matter how great sinners they have been; for, as the Saints say, never has it been heard since the world was the world, that any one has confidently and perseveringly had recourse to our Blessed Lady, and yet has been repelled.

She is so powerful that never have any of her petitions been refused. She has but to show herself before her Son to pray to Him, and straightway He grants her desires, straightway He receives her prayers. He is always lovingly vanquished by the breasts, the yearnings, and the prayers of His dearest Mother. All this is drawn from St. Bernard and from St. Bonaventure, so that, according to them, we have three steps to mount to go to God: the first, which is the nearest to us, and the most suited to our capacity, is Mary; the second is Jesus Christ; and the third is God the Father. To go to Jesus, we must go to Mary; she is our mediatrix of intercession. To go to God the Father, we must go to Jesus; for He is our Mediator of redemption. Now it is by the devotion which I am about to bring forward, that this order is guarded perfectly.

Fifth Truth

It is very difficult, considering our weakness and frailty, to preserve in ourselves the graces and treasures which we have received from God:

1. Because we have this treasure, which is worth more than heaven and earth put together, in frail vessels (*Habemus thesaurum istum in vasis fictilibus,*—"We have this treasure in earthen vessels"), in a corruptible body, and in a weak and inconstant soul, which a mere nothing disturbs and dejects.

2. Because the devils, who are skilful thieves, wish to surprise us unawares, and to strip us. They watch day and night for the favourable moment. For that end they go round about us incessantly to devour us, and to snatch from us in one moment, by a sin, all that we have gained of graces and of merits for many years. Their malice, their experience, their stratagems, and their number, ought to make us fear immensely this misfortune, especially when we see how many persons, fuller of grace than we are, richer in virtues, better founded in experience, and far higher exalted in sanctity, have been surprised, robbed, and unhappily pillaged. Ah! how many of the cedars of Lebanon, how many of the stars of the firmament, have we not seen to fall miserably, and in the twinkling of an eye to lose all their height and all their brightness! Whence comes that sad and curious change? It has not been for want of grace, which is wanting to no man; but it has been want of humility. They thought themselves stronger and more sufficient than they were. They thought themselves capable of guarding their own treasures. They trusted in themselves, leaned upon themselves. They thought their house secure enough, and their coffers strong enough, to keep the precious treasure of their grace. It is because of that scarcely sensible leaning upon themselves, while all the while it seemed to them that they were leaning only on the grace of God, that the most just Lord has permitted them to be robbed by leaving them to themselves. Alas! if they had but known the admirable devotion which I will unfold presently, they would have confided their treasure to a Virgin, powerful and faithful, who would have kept it for them as if it had been her own possession; nay, who would have even taken it as an obligation of justice on herself to preserve it for them.

3. It is difficult to persevere in justice because of the strange corruption of the world. The world is now so corrupt, that it seems to be inevitable that religious hearts should be soiled, if not by its mud, at least by its dust. So that it has become a kind of miracle for any one to remain firm in the midst of this impetuous torrent without being drawn in by it, in the midst of that stormy sea without being drowned in it or stripped by the pirates and the corsairs, in the midst of that pestilent air without being infected by it. It is the Virgin, alone faithful, in whom the serpent has never had part, who works this miracle for those who serve her in that sweet way which I have shortly to unfold.

Having assumed these Five Truths, we must now take more pains than ever to make a good choice of the true devotion to our Blessed Lady. There are at this time, more than ever, false devotions to our Blessed Lady, which it is easy to mistake for true ones. The devil, like a false coiner and a subtle and experienced sharper, has already deceived and destroyed so many souls by a false devotion to the Blessed Virgin, that he makes a daily use of his diabolical experience to plunge many others by this same way into everlasting perdition; amusing them, lulling them to sleep in sin, under the pretext of some prayers badly said, or of some outward practices which he inspires. As a false coiner does not ordinarily counterfeit any thing but gold and silver, or very rarely the other metals, because they are not worth the trouble, so the evil spirit does not for the most part counterfeit the other devotions, but only those to Jesus and Mary, the devotion to Holy Communion, and to our Blessed Lady, because they are, among other devotions, what gold and silver are amongst metals.

It is, then, very important first of all to know false devotions to our Blessed Lady in order to avoid them; and secondly the true devotion in order to embrace it. In conclusion, among so many practices of true devotion to our Blessed Lady, I will explain more in detail, in the second part of this treatise, which is the most perfect one, the one most agreeable to our Lady, the most glorious to God , and the most sanctifying to ourselves, in order that we may attach ourselves to it.

CHAPTER 3

Discernment of False Devotions to Our Lady

I find seven kinds of false devotees and false devotions to our Lady, namely, (1) the *critical* devotees; (2) the *scrupulous* devotees; (3) the *external* devotees; (4) the *presumptuous* devotees; (5) the *inconstant* devotees; (6) the *hypocritical* devotees; and (7) the *interested* devotees.

The **critical** devotees are, for the most part, proud scholars, rash and self-sufficient spirits, who have at bottom some devotion to the holy Virgin, but who criticise nearly all the practices of devotion to her, which the simple people pay simply and holily to their good Mother, because these practices do not fall in with their own humour and fancy. They call in doubt all the miracles and histories recorded by authors worthy of our faith, or drawn from the chronicles of religious orders; narratives which testify to us the mercies and the power of the most holy Virgin. They cannot see without uneasiness simple and humble people on their knees before an altar or an image of our Lady, sometimes in the corner of a street, in order to pray to God there; and they even accuse them of idolatry, as if they adored the wood or the stone. They say that, for their part, they are not fond of these external devotions, and that their minds are not so weak as to give faith to such a number of tales and little histories as are in circulation about our Lady. Or, at other times, they reply that the narrators have spoken as professional orators, with exaggeration; or they put a bad interpretation upon their words. These kind of false devotees and of proud and worldly people are greatly to be feared. They do an infinite wrong to the devotion to our Lady; and they are but too successful in alienating people from it, under the pretext of destroying its abuses.

The **scrupulous** devotees are those who fear to dishonour the Son by honouring the Mother, to abase the one in elevating the other. They cannot bear that we should attribute to our Lady the most just praises which the holy Fathers have given her. It is all they can do to endure that there should be more people before the altar of the Blessed Virgin than before the Blessed Sacrament, as if the one was contrary to the other, as if those who prayed to our Blessed Lady did not pray to Jesus Christ by her. They are unwilling that we should speak so often of our Lady, and address ourselves so frequently to her. These are the favourite sentences constantly in their mouths: "To what end are so many chaplets, so many confraternities, and so many external devotions to the Blessed Virgin? There is much of ignorance in all this. It makes a mummery of our religion. Speak to us of those who are devout to Jesus Christ" (yet they often name Him without uncovering: I say this by way of parenthesis). "We must have recourse to Jesus Christ; He is our only Mediator. We must preach Jesus Christ; this is the solid devotion." What they say is true in a certain sense, but it is very dangerous, when, by the application they make of it, they hinder devotion to our Blessed Lady, and it is, under the pretext of a greater good, a subtle snare of the evil one. For never do we honour Jesus Christ more than when we are most honouring His Blessed Mother. Indeed we only honour Mary that we may the more perfectly honour Jesus, inasmuch as we only go to her as to the way in which we are to find the end we are seeking, which is Jesus.

> *"Blessed art thou amongst women, and blessed is the fruit of thy womb, Jesus."*

The Church, with the Holy Ghost, blesses our Lady first, and our Lord second: *Benedicta tu in mulieribus, et benedictus fructus ventris tui Jesus,*— "Blessed art thou amongst women, and blessed is the fruit of thy womb, Jesus." It is not that Mary is more than Jesus, or even equal to Him. That would be an intolerable heresy; but it is that, in order to bless Jesus more perfectly, we must begin by blessing Mary. Let us, then, say with all the true clients of our Lady against these false scrupulous devotees, O Mary, thou art blessed amongst all women, and blessed is the fruit of thy womb, Jesus.

External devotees are persons who make all devotion to our Blessed Lady consist in outward practices. They have no taste except for the exterior of this devotion, because they have no interior spirit of their own. They will say quantities of Rosaries with the greatest precipitation; they will hear many Masses distractedly; they will go without devotion to processions; they will enrol themselves in all sorts of confraternities, without amending their lives, without doing any violence to their passions, or without imitating the virtues of that most holy Virgin. They have no love but for the sensible part of devotion, without having any relish for its solidity. If they have not sensible sweetness in their practices, they think they are doing nothing; they get all out of joint, throw every thing up, or do every thing at random. The world is full of these exterior devotees; and there are no people who are more critical of men of prayer, of those who foster an interior spirit as the essential thing, while they do not lightly account of that outward modesty which always accompanies true devotion.

Presumptuous devotees are sinners abandoned to their passions, or lovers of the world, who, under the fair name of Christians and clients of our Blessed Lady, conceal pride, avarice, impurity, drunkenness, anger, swearing, detraction, injustice, or some other sin. They sleep in peace in the midst of their bad habits, without doing any violence to themselves to correct their faults, under the pretext that they are devout to the Blessed Virgin. They promise themselves that God will pardon them; that they will not be allowed to die without confession; and that they will not be lost eternally, because they say the Rosary, because they fast on Saturdays, because they belong to the Confraternity of the Holy Rosary, or wear the scapular, or are enrolled in other congregations, or wear the little habit or little chain of our Lady.[1] They will not believe us when we tell them that their devotion is only an illusion of the devil, and a pernicious presumption likely to destroy their souls. They say that God is good and merciful; that He has not made us to condemn us everlastingly; that no man is without sin; that they shall not die without confession; that one good Peccavi at the hour of death is enough; that they are devout to our Lady; that they wear the scapular; and that they say daily, without reproach or vanity, seven Paters and Aves in her honour; and that they sometimes say the Rosary and the Office of our Lady, besides fasting, and other things. To give authority to all this, and to blind themselves still further, they quote certain stories, which they have heard or read,—it does not matter to them whether they be true or false,—relating how people have died in mortal sin without confession; and then, because in their lifetime they sometimes said some prayers, or went through some practices of devotion to our Lady, how they have been raised to life again, in order to go to confession, or their soul been miraculously retained in their bodies till confession; or how they have obtained from God at the moment of death

---

1. See note on page 72.

contrition and pardon of their sins, and so have been saved; and that they themselves expect similar favours. Nothing in Christianity is more detestable than this diabolical presumption. For how can we say truly that we love and honour our Blessed Lady, when by our sins we are pitilessly piercing, wounding, crucifying, and outraging Jesus Christ her Son? If Mary laid down a law to herself, to save by her mercy this sort of people, she would be authorising crime, and assisting to crucify and outrage her Son. Who would dare to think such a thought as that?

I say, that thus to abuse devotion to our Lady, which, after devotion to our Lord in the Blessed Sacrament, is the holiest and solidest of all devotions, is to be guilty of a horrible sacrilege, which, after the sacrilege of an unworthy Communion, is the greatest and the least pardonable of all sacrileges.

I confess that, in order to be truly devout to our Blessed Lady, it is not absolutely necessary to be so holy as to avoid every sin, though this were to be wished; but so much at least is necessary, and I beg you, to lay it well to heart:

1. To have a sincere resolution to avoid, at least, all mortal sin, which outrages the Mother as well as the Son. 2. I would add also that to do violence to ourselves to avoid sin, to enrol ourselves in confraternities, to say the Rosary or other prayers, to fast on Saturdays, and the like, is wonderfully useful to the conversion of a sinner, however hardened; and if my reader, is such a one, even if he has his foot in the abyss, I would counsel these things to him. Nevertheless it must be on the condition that he will only practise these good works with the intention of obtaining from God, by the intercession of the Blessed Virgin, the grace of contrition and the pardon of his sins, to conquer his evil habits, and not to remain quietly in the state of sin, in spite of the remorse of his conscience, the example of Jesus Christ and the Saints, and the maxims of the holy Gospel.

The **inconstant** devotees are those who are devout to our Blessed Lady by intervals and whims. Sometimes they are fervent and sometimes lukewarm. Sometimes they seem ready to do any thing for her, and then, a little afterwards, they are not like the same people. They begin by taking up all the devotions to her, and enrolling themselves in the confraternities; and then they do not practise the rules with fidelity. They change like the moon; and Mary puts them under her feet with the crescent, because they are mutable, and unworthy to be reckoned among the servants of that faithful Virgin, whose clients have for their special graces fidelity and constancy.

It were better for such persons to load themselves with fewer prayers and practices, and to fulfil them with faithfulness and love, in spite of the world, the devil, and the flesh.

We have still to mention the false devotees to our Blessed Lady, who are the ***hypocritical*** devotees; who cloak their sins and sinful habits under her mantle, in order to pass in the eyes of men for what they are not.

There are also the ***interested*** devotees, who have recourse to our Lady only to gain some lawsuit, or to avoid some danger, or to be cured of some illness, or for some other similar necessity, without which they would forget her altogether. Both, however, of these two last classes are false devotees, and neither of them pass current before God and His holy Mother.

Let us, then, take great care not to be of the number of the *critical* devotees, who believe nothing and criticise every thing; nor of the *scrupulous* devotees, who are afraid of being too devout to our Lady, out of respect to our Lord; nor of the *exterior* devotees, who make all their devotion consist in outward practices; nor of the *presumptuous* devotees, who, under the pretext of their false devotion to the Blessed Virgin, wallow in their sins; nor of the *inconstant* devotees, who by levity change their practices of devotion, or throw them up altogether on the least temptation; nor of the *hypocritical* devotees, who put themselves into confraternities, and wear the liveries of the Blessed Virgin, in order to pass for good people; nor, finally, of the *interested* devotees, who only have recourse to our Lady to be delivered from bodily evils, or to obtain temporal goods.

Statue depicting St. Louis de Montfort offering his *Treatise on True Devotion to Mary* to Our Lady as Queen of All Hearts, Chapel of the Missionaries of the Company of Mary (Montfort Missionaries), Rome, Italy.

CHAPTER 4

Characteristics of True Devotion

After having laid bare and condemned the false devotions to the most holy Virgin, we must, in a few words, characterise the true devotion. It must be (1) *interior*, (2) *tender*, (3) *holy*, (4) *constant*, and (5) *disinterested*.

True devotion to our Lady is *interior*; that is to say, it comes from the spirit and the heart. It flows from the esteem we have of her, the high idea we have formed of her greatness, and the love which we have for her.

It is *tender*; that is to say, full of confidence in her, like a child's confidence in his loving mother. This confidence makes the soul have recourse to her in all its bodily or mental necessities, with much simplicity, trust, and tenderness. It implores the aid of its good Mother, at all times, in all places, and about all things; in its doubts, that it may be enlightened; in its wanderings, that it may be brought into the right path; in its temptations, that it may be supported; in its weaknesses, that it may be strengthened; in its falls, that it may be lifted up; in its discouragements, that it may be cheered; in its scruples, that they may be taken away; in its crosses, toils, and disappointments of life, that it may be consoled under them. In a word, in all its evils of body and mind, the soul's ordinary refuge is in Mary, without fearing to be importunate to her or to displease Jesus Christ.

True devotion to our Lady is *holy*; that is to say, it leads the soul to avoid sin, and to imitate in the Blessed Virgin particularly her profound humility, her lively faith, her continual prayer, her universal mortification, her divine purity, her ardent charity, her heroic patience, her angelical sweetness, and her divine wisdom. These are the ten principal virtues of the most holy Virgin.

True devotion to our Lady is *constant*. It confirms the soul in good, and it does not let it easily abandon its spiritual exercises. It makes it courageous in opposing the world in its fashions and maxims, the flesh in its wearinesses and passions, and the devil in his temptations. So that a person truly devout to our Blessed Lady is neither changeable, irritable, scrupulous, nor timid. It is not that such a person does not fall, or change sometimes in the sensible feeling of devotion, or in the amount of devotion itself. But when he falls, he rises again by stretching out his hand to his good Mother. If he loses the taste and relish of devotion, he does not disturb himself because of that; for the just and faithful client of Mary lives on the faith of Jesus and Mary, and not on sentiments and sensibilities.

Lastly, true devotion to our Blessed Lady is **disinterested**; that is to say, it inspires the soul not to seek itself but God only, and God in His holy Mother. A true client of Mary does not serve that august Queen from a spirit of lucre and interest, nor for its own good, whether temporal, corporal, or spiritual; but exclusively because she merits to be served, and God alone in her. He does not love Mary precisely because she does him good, or because he hopes in her; but because she is so worthy of love. It is on this account that he loves and serves her as faithfully in his disgusts and drynesses, as in his sweetnesses and sensible fervours. He loves her as much on Calvary, as at the marriage of Cana. Oh! how such a client of our Blessed Lady, who has no self-seeking in his service of her, is agreeable and precious in the eyes of God and of His holy Mother! But in these days how rare is such a sight! It is that it may be less rare that I have taken my pen to put on paper what I have taught, in public and in private, during my missions for many years.

I have now said many things about the most holy Virgin; but I have many more to say, and there are infinitely more which I shall omit, whether from ignorance, inability, or want of time, in the design which I have to form a true client of Mary, and a true disciple of Jesus Christ.

Oh! but my labour will have been well expended if this little Writing, falling into the hands of a soul of good dispositions, a soul well born,—born of God and of Mary, and not of blood, nor of the will of the flesh, nor of the will of man,—should unfold to him, and should, by the grace of the Holy Ghost, inspire him with, the excellence and the price of that true and solid devotion to our Blessed Lady, which I am going presently to describe. If I knew that my guilty blood could serve in engraving upon any one's heart the truths which I am writing in honour of my true Mother and sovereign Mistress, I would use my blood instead of ink to form the letters, in the hope to find some good souls who, by their fidelity to the practice which I teach, shall compensate to my dear Mother and Mistress for the losses which she has suffered through my ingratitude and infidelities. I feel myself more than ever animated to believe and to hope all which I have had deeply engraven upon my heart, and have asked of God these many years, namely, that sooner or later the Blessed Virgin shall have more children, servants, and slaves of love than ever; and that, by this means, Jesus Christ, my dear Master, shall reign more in hearts than ever.

I clearly foresee that raging beasts shall come in fury to tear with their diabolical teeth this little Writing and him whom the Holy Ghost has made use of to write it, or at least to smother it in the silence of a coffer, that it may not appear. They shall even attack and persecute those who shall read it and carry it out in practice. But what matter? On the contrary, so much the better! This very foresight encourages me, and makes me hope for a great success; that is to say, for a great squadron of brave and valiant soldiers of Jesus and Mary, of both sexes, to combat the world, the devil, and corrupted nature in those more than ever perilous times which are about to come! *Qui legit, intelligat. Qui potest capere, capiat,*—"He who reads, let him understand. He who can receive it, let him receive it."

PART II

On the Most Excellent Devotion to Our Blessed Lady,
or the Perfect Consecration to Jesus by Mary

Statue of Our Lady of Fatima carried in procession during a Public Square Rosary Rally in New York City, October 13, 2012.

CHAPTER 5

Preliminary Observations on the Different Ways of Honouring Our Blessed Lady

Interior Practices

There are several interior practices of true devotion to the Blessed Virgin. Here are the principal of them stated compendiously. **1.** To honour her as the worthy Mother of God, with the worship of hyperdulia; that is to say, to esteem her and honour her above all the other Saints, as the masterpiece of grace, and the first after Jesus Christ, true God and true Man; **2.** to meditate her virtues, her privileges, and her actions; **3.** to contemplate her grandeurs; **4.** to make to her acts of love, of praise, of gratitude; **5.** to invoke her cordially; **6.** to offer ourselves to her, and unite ourselves with her; **7.** to do all our actions with the view of pleasing her; **8.** to begin, to continue, and to finish all our actions by her, in her, and with her, in order that we may do them by Jesus Christ, in Jesus Christ, with Jesus Christ, and for Jesus Christ our Last End. We will presently explain this last practice.

Exterior Practices

True devotion to our Lady has also several exterior practices, of which the following are the chief: **1.** to enrol ourselves in her confraternities, and enter her congregations; **2.** to join the religious orders instituted in her honour; **3.** to publish her praises; **4.** to give alms, to fast, and to undergo outward and inward mortifications in her honour; **5.** to wear her liveries, such as the rosary, the scapular, or the little chain; **6.** to recite with attention, devotion, and modesty, the holy Rosary, composed of fifteen decades of Hail Marys in honour of the fifteen principal mysteries of Jesus Christ, or five decades, which is the third of the Rosary, either in honour of the five Joyous Mysteries, which are the Annunciation, the Visitation, the Nativity of Jesus Christ, the Purification, and the Finding of our Lord in the Temple; or in honour of the five Sorrowful Mysteries, which are the Agony of our Lord in the Garden of Olives, His Scourging, His Crowning with Thorns, His Carrying of the Cross, and His Crucifixion; or in honour of the five Glorious Mysteries, which are the Resurrection of Jesus Christ, the Ascension, the Descent of the Holy Ghost at Pentecost, the Assumption of our Blessed Lady body and soul into Heaven, and her Coronation by the Three Persons of the Most Holy Trinity. We may also say a Chaplet of six or seven decades in honour of the years which we believe our Lady lived on earth; or the little Corona of the Blessed Virgin, composed of three Our Fathers and twelve Hail Marys, in honour of her crown of twelve stars, or privileges; or the Office of our Lady, so universally received and recited in the Church; or the Little Psalter of the holy Virgin, which St. Bonaventure has composed in her honour, and which is so tender and so devout that one cannot say it without being melted by it; or fourteen Our Fathers and Hail Marys in honour of her fourteen joys; or some other prayers, hymns, and canticles of the Church, such as the *Salve Regina*, the *Alma,* the *Ave Regina cœlorum*, or the *Regina cœli*, according to the different seasons; or the *Ave Maris stella*, the *O gloriosa Domina*, the *Magnificat*, or some other practices of devotion of which books are full; **7.** to sing or have sung spiritual canticles in her honour; **8.** to make her a number of genuflexions or reverences, while saying, for example, every morning, sixty or a hundred times *Ave Maria, Virgo fidelis*, to obtain from God the grace by her to be faithful to the graces of God during the day; and then again in the evening, *Ave Maria, Mater misericordiæ*, to ask pardon of God by her for the sins that we have committed during the day; **9.** to take care of her confraternities, to adorn her altars, to crown and ornament her images; **10.** to carry her images, or to have them carried, in procession, and to carry a picture or image of her about our own persons, as a mighty arm against the evil spirit; **11.** to have her images or her name carved, and placed in churches, or in houses, or on the gates and entrances into cities, churches, and houses; **12.** to consecrate ourselves to her in a special and solemn manner.

There are a quantity of other practices of true devotion towards the Blessed Virgin which the Holy Ghost has inspired into saintly souls, and which are very sanctifying; they can be read at length in the *Paradise Opened* of Fr. Barry, the Jesuit, where he has collected a great number of devotions which the Saints have practised in honour of our Lady, devotions which serve marvellously to sanctify souls, provided they are performed as they ought to be; that is to say, (1) with a good and pure intention to please God only, to unite ourselves to Jesus Christ as to our Last End, and to edify our neighbour; (2) with attention, and without voluntary distraction; (3) with devotion, equally avoiding precipitation or negligence; (4) with modesty, and a respectful and edifying care of the postures of the body.

But after all, I loudly protest that, having read nearly all the books which profess to treat of devotion to our Lady, and having conversed familiarly and holily with the best and wisest of men of these latter times, I have never known nor heard any practice of devotion towards her at all equal to the one which I wish now to unfold; exacting from the soul as it does more sacrifices for God, emptying the soul more of itself and of its self-love, keeping it more faithfully in grace, and grace more faithfully in it, uniting it more perfectly and more easily to Jesus Christ; and finally, being more glorious to God, more sanctifying to the soul, and more useful to our neighbour, than any other of the devotions to her.

As the essential of this devotion consists in the interior which it ought to form, it will not be equally comprehended by every body. Some will stop at what is exterior in it, and will go no further, and these will be the greatest number. Some, in small number, will enter into its inward spirit; but they will only mount but one step. Who will mount to the second step? Who will get as far as the third? Lastly, who will so advance as to make this devotion his habitual *state*? He alone to whom the spirit of Jesus Christ shall have revealed the secret, the faultlessly faithful soul, whom He shall conduct there Himself, to advance from virtue to virtue, from grace to grace, from light to light, until he arrives at the transformation of himself into Jesus Christ, and to the plenitude of His age on earth, and of His glory in heaven.

"Cristo de la Sentencia." Christ is sentenced in the prætorium of Pilate. Detail of a Holy Week float depicting the scene, Seville, Spain.

CHAPTER 6

In What Consists the Perfect
Consecration to Jesus Christ

All our perfection consists in being conformed, united, and consecrated to Jesus Christ; and therefore the most perfect of all devotions is, without any doubt, that which the most perfectly conforms, unites, and consecrates us to Jesus Christ. Now, Mary being the most conformed of all creatures to Jesus Christ, it follows that, of all devotions, that which most consecrates and conforms the soul to our Lord is devotion to His holy Mother, and that the more a soul is consecrated to Mary, the more is it consecrated to Jesus. Hence it comes to pass, that the most perfect consecration to Jesus Christ is nothing else but a perfect and entire consecration of ourselves to the Blessed Virgin, and this is the devotion which I teach; or in other words, a perfect renewal of the vows and promises of holy Baptism.

This devotion consists, then, in giving ourselves entirely and altogether to our Lady, in order to belong entirely and altogether to Jesus by her. We must give her (1) our body, with all its senses and its members; (2) our soul, with all its powers; (3) the exterior goods of fortune, whether present or to come; (4) our interior and spiritual goods, which are our merits and our virtues, and our good works, past, present, and future. In a word, we must give her all we have in the order of nature and in the order of grace, and all that may become ours in future in the orders of nature, grace, and glory; and this we must do without any reserve of so much as one farthing, one hair, or one least good action; and we must do it also for all eternity, and we must do it further without pretending to, or hoping for, any other recompense for our offering and service, except the honour of belonging to Jesus Christ by Mary and in Mary, even though that sweet Mistress were not, as she always is, the most generous and the most grateful of creatures.

Here we must remark, that there are two things in the good works which we do, namely, satisfaction and merit; in other words, their satisfactory or impetratory value, and their meritorious value. The satisfactory or impetratory value of a good work is the good action, so far as it satisfies for the pain due to sin, or obtains some fresh increase of grace; the meritorious value, or the merit, is the good action, so far as it merits grace now and eternal glory hereafter. Now, in this consecration of ourselves to our Lady, we give her all the satisfactory, impetratory, and meritorious value of our actions; in other words, the satisfactions and merits of all our good works. We give her all our merits, graces, and virtues, not to communicate them to others,—for our merits, graces, and virtues are, properly speaking, incommunicable, and it is only Jesus Christ, who, in making Himself our surety with His Father, is able to communicate His merits,—but we give her them to keep them, augment them, and embellish them for us, as we shall explain by and by. But we give her our satisfactions to communicate them to whom she likes, and for the greatest glory of God.

It follows from this, that

1. by this devotion, we give to Jesus Christ, in the most perfect manner, inasmuch as it is by Mary's hands, all we can give Him, and far more than by any other devotions, in which we give Him either part of our time, or a part of our good works, or a part of our satisfactions and mortifications; whereas here every thing is given and consecrated to Him, even to the right of disposing of our interior goods, and of the satisfactions which we gain by our good works daily. This is more than we do even in a religious order. In religious orders we give God the goods of fortune by the vow of poverty, the goods of the body by the vow of chastity, our own will by the vow of obedience, and sometimes the liberty of the body by the vow of cloister. But we do not by those vows give Him the liberty or the right to dispose of the value of our good works; and we do not strip ourselves, as far as a Christian man can do so, of that which is dearest and most precious to Him, namely, his merits and satisfactions.

2. A person who is thus voluntarily consecrated and sacrificed to Jesus Christ by Mary can no longer dispose of the value of any of his good actions. All he suffers, all he thinks, all the good he says or does, belongs to Mary, in order that she may dispose of it according to the will of her Son, and His greatest glory, without, however, that dependence prejudicing in any way the obligations of the state we may be in at present, or may be placed in for the future; for example, without prejudicing the obligations of a priest, who, by his office or otherwise, ought to apply the satisfactory or impetratory value of the holy Mass to some

private person; for we make the offering of this devotion only according to the order of God and the duties of our state.

3. We consecrate ourselves at one and the same time to the most holy Virgin and to Jesus Christ: to the most holy Virgin, as to the perfect means which Jesus Christ has chosen, whereby to unite Himself to us, and us to Him; and to our Lord, as to our Last End, to whom we owe all we are, as our Redeemer and our God.

I have said that this devotion may most justly be called a perfect renewal of the vows or promises of holy Baptism. For every Christian, before his Baptism, was the slave of the devil, seeing that he belonged to him. He has in his Baptism, by his own mouth or by his sponsor's, solemnly renounced Satan, his pomps and his works; and he has taken Jesus Christ for his Master and Sovereign Lord, to depend upon Him in the quality of a slave of love. This is what we do by the present devotion. We renounce, as is expressed in the formula of consecration, the devil, the world, sin, and self; and we give ourselves entirely to Jesus Christ by the hands of Mary. Nay, we even do something more; for in Baptism, we ordinarily speak by the mouth of another, namely, by our godfather or godmother, and so we give ourselves, voluntarily, knowing what we are doing. Moreover, in holy Baptism, we do not give ourselves to Jesus by the hands of Mary, at least not in an expressed manner; and we do not give Him the value of our good actions. We remain entirely free after Baptism, either to apply them to whom we please or to keep them for ourselves. But, by this devotion, we give ourselves to our Lord expressly by the hands of Mary, and we consecrate to Him the value of all our actions.

Men, says St. Thomas, make a vow at their Baptism to renounce the devil and all his pomps,—*In Baptismo vovent homines abrenuntiare diabolo et pompis ejus.* This vow, says St. Augustine, is the greatest and most indispensable of all vows,—*Votum maximum nostrum, quo vovimus nos in Christo esse mansuros."* It is thus also that canonists speak: *Præcipuum votum est, quod in Baptismate facimus,*—"The chief of vows is the one we make at Baptism." Yet who has kept this great vow? Who is it that faithfully performs the promises of holy Baptism? Have not almost all Christians swerved from the loyalty which they promised Jesus in their Baptism? Whence can come this universal disobedience, except from oblivion of the promises and engagements of holy Baptism, and from the fact that hardly any one ratifies of himself the contract he made with God by those who stood sponsors for him? This is so true, that the Council of Sens, convoked by order of Louis the Débonnaire to remedy the disorders of Christians, which were then so great, judged that the principal cause of that corruption of morals arose from the oblivion and ignorance in which men lived of the engagements of holy Baptism; and it could think of no better means for remedying so great an evil than to persuade Christians to renew the vows and promises of Baptism.

The Catechism of the Council of Trent, the faithful interpreter of that holy Council, exhorts the parish-priests to do the same thing; and to induce the people to remember themselves, and to believe that they are bound and consecrated to our Lord Jesus Christ, as slaves to their Redeemer and Lord. These are its words: "*Parochus fidelem ad eam rationem cohortabitur ut sciat æquissimum esse...nos ipsos non secus ac mancipio Redemptori nostro ac Domino in perpetuum addicere et consecrare.*" (Cat. Conc. Trid. Par. 1, c. 3, sec. 4)

Now if the Councils, the Fathers, and experience even, show us that the best means of remedying the irregularities of Christians is by making them call to mind the obligations of their Baptism, and persuading them to renew now the vows they made then, does it not stand to reason that we shall do it in a perfect manner, by this devotion and consecration of ourselves to our Lord, through His holy Mother? I say in a perfect manner; because in thus consecrating ourselves to Him we make use of the most perfect of all means, namely, the Blessed Virgin.

No one can object to this devotion as either a new or an indifferent one

It is not new; because the Councils, the Fathers, and many authors both ancient and modern, speak of this consecration to our Lord, in renewing the vows and promises of Baptism, as of a thing anciently practised, and which they counsel to all Christians. Neither is it a matter of indifference; because the principal source of all disorders, and consequently of the eternal perdition of Christians, comes from their forgetfulness and indifference about this practice. But some may object that this devotion, in making us give to our Lord by our Lady's hands the value of all our good works, prayers, mortifications, and alms, puts us into a state of incapacity for succouring the souls of our parents, friends, and benefactors.

I answer them as follows:

1. That it is not credible that our parents, friends, and benefactors, should suffer any damage from the fact of our being devoted and consecrated without exception to the service of our Lord and His holy Mother. To think this, would be to think unworthily of the goodness and power of Jesus and Mary, who know well how to assist our parents, friends, and benefactors out of our own little spiritual revenue, or by other ways.

2. This practice does not hinder us from praying for others, whether dead or living, although the application of our good works depends on the will of our Blessed Lady. On the contrary, it is this very thing which will lead us to pray with more confidence; just as a rich person, who has given all his wealth to his prince, in order to honour him the more, would beg the prince all the more confidently to give an alms to one of his friends who should demand it. It would even be conferring a fresh favour on the prince, and giving him a fresh pleasure, to give him an occasion of testifying his gratitude towards a person who stripped himself to clothe him, and who impoverished himself to honour him. We must say the same of our Blessed Lord and of our Lady. They will never let themselves be overcome in gratitude. Some one, perhaps, may say, "If I give to our Blessed Lady all the value of my actions to apply to whom she wills, I shall have to suffer, perhaps, a long time in Purgatory." This objection, which comes from self-love and ignorance of the generosity of God and His holy Mother, demolishes itself. A fervent and generous soul, who prizes the interests of God more than his own; who gives God all he has, without reserve, so that he can do nothing more; who breathes only the glory and reign of Jesus Christ by His holy Mother, and who makes an entire sacrifice of himself to bring it about,—will this generous and liberal soul, I say, be more punished in the other world because it has been more liberal and more disinterested than others? Far, indeed, will that be from the truth! It is towards that soul, as we shall see in conclusion, that our Lord and His holy Mother are most liberal in this world and in the other, in the orders of nature, grace, and glory.

But we must now, as briefly as we can, run over the motives which ought to recommend this devotion to us, the marvellous effects it produces in the souls of the faithful, and its practices.

Table at which St. Louis de Montfort wrote his *Treatise on True Devotion to Mary*, Saint-Laurent-sur-Sèvre, France.

CHAPTER 7

Motives of this Perfect Consecration

First Motive

The first motive, which shows us the excellence of this consecration of ourselves by the hands of Mary. If we can conceive on earth no employment more lofty than the service of God,—if the least servant of God is richer, more powerful, and more noble, than all the kings and emperors of this earth, unless they also are the servants of God,—what must be the riches, the power, and the dignity, of the faithful and perfect servant of God, who is devoted to His service entirely and without reserve, to the utmost extent that is possible! Such is the faithful and loving slave of Jesus in Mary, who has given himself up utterly to the service of that King of kings, by the hands of His holy Mother, and has reserved nothing for himself. Not all the gold of earth, nor all the beauties of the heavens, can repay him.

The other congregations, associations, and confraternities, erected in honour of our Lord and His holy Mother, and which do such immense good in Christendom, do not make us give every thing without reserve. They only prescribe to their members certain practices and actions to satisfy their obligations. They leave them free for all the other actions and times of their lives. But this devotion makes us give to Jesus and Mary, without reserve, all our thoughts, words, actions, and sufferings, all the times of our life, in such sort that whether we wake or sleep, whether we eat or drink, whether we do great actions or very little ones, it is always true to say that whatever we do, even without thinking of it, is, by virtue of our offering, at least if it has not been expressly retracted, done for Jesus and Mary. What a consolation is this!

Moreover, as I have already said, there is no other practice equal to this for enabling us to get rid with facility of a certain proprietorship, which imperceptibly insinuates itself into our best actions. Our good Jesus gives us this great grace in recompense for the heroic and disinterested action of making a cession to Him, by the hands of His holy Mother, of all the value of our good works. If He gives a hundredfold even in this world to those who for His love quit outward and temporal and perishable goods, what will that hundredfold be which He will give to the man who sacrifices for Him even his inward and spiritual goods!

Jesus, our great friend, has given Himself to us without reserve, body and soul, virtues, graces, and merits. *Se toto totum me comparavit,* said St. Bernard,—"He has bought the whole of me by the whole of Himself." Is it not, then, a simple matter of justice and of gratitude that we should give him all that we can give Him? He has been the first to be liberal towards us; let us, at least, be the second; and then, in life and death, and throughout all eternity, we shall find Him still more liberal. *Cum liberali liberalis erit,*—"With the liberal He will be liberal."

Second Motive

The second motive, which shows us how just it is in itself, and advantageous to Christians, to consecrate themselves entirely to the Blessed Virgin by this practice, in order to belong more perfectly to Jesus Christ.

This good Master has not disdained to shut Himself up in the womb of the Blessed Virgin, as a captive and as a loving slave, and to be subject and obedient to her for thirty years. It is here, I repeat it, that the human mind loses itself when it seriously reflects on the conduct of the Incarnate Wisdom, who has not willed, though He might have done so, to give Himself to men directly, but through the Blessed Virgin. He did not will to come into the world at the age of a perfect man, independent of others, but like a poor and little babe, dependent on the cares and nourishment of this holy Mother. He is that Infinite Wisdom, who had a boundless desire to glorify God His Father, and to save men; and yet He found no more perfect means, no shorter way to do it, than to submit Himself in all things to the Blessed Virgin, not only during the first eight, ten, or fifteen years of His life, like other children, but for thirty years! He gave more glory to God His Father during all that time of submission and dependence to our Blessed Lady than He would have given Him if He had employed those thirty years in working miracles, in preaching to the whole earth, and in converting all men, seeing that His heavenly Father and Himself had ruled it thus: *Quæ placita sunt ei, facio semper,*—"I always do the things which please Him." Oh! how highly we glorify God, when, after the example of Jesus, we submit ourselves to Mary!

Having, then, before our eyes the example so plain and so well known to the whole world, are we so senseless as to imagine that we can find a more perfect or shorter means of glorifying God than that of submitting ourselves to Mary, after the example of her Son? Let us recall here, as a proof of the dependence we ought to have on our Blessed Lady, what I have said above in bringing forward the example which the Father, the Son, and the Holy Ghost give to this dependence. The Father has not given, and does not give, His Son except by her; He has no children but by her, and communicates no graces but by her. God the Son has not been formed for the whole world in general except by her; and He is not daily formed and engendered except by her, in the union with the Holy Ghost; neither does He communicate His merits and His virtues except by her. The Holy Ghost has not formed Jesus Christ except by her; neither does He form the members of our Lord's Mystical Body except by her; and through her alone does He dispense His favours and His gifts. After so many and such pressing examples of the Most Holy Trinity, can we, without an extreme blindness, dispense ourselves from Mary, and not consecrate ourselves to her, and depend on her to go to God, and to sacrifice ourselves to God?

Here are some Latin passages of the Fathers, which I have chosen to prove what has just been said:

- *"Duo filii Mariæ sunt, homo Deus et homo purus, unius corporaliter, et alterius spiritualiter Mater est Maria."*
  —St. Bonaventure and Origen

- *"Hæc est voluntas Dei, qui totum nos voluit habere per Mariam, ac proinde si quid spei, si quid gratiæ, si quid salutis, ab ea noverimus redundare."* —St. Bernard

- *"Omnia dona, virtutes gratiæ ipsius Spiritus Sancti, quibus vult, et quandò vult, quomodò vult, et quantùm vult, per ipsius manus administrantur."* —St. Bernardine

- *"Quia indignus eras cui donaretur, datum est Mariæ, ut per illam acciperes quidquid haberes."* —St. Bernard

God, says St. Bernard, seeing that we are unworthy to receive His graces immediately from His own hand, gives them to Mary, in order that we may have through her whatever He wills to give us; and He also finds His glory in receiving through the hands of Mary the gratitude, respect, and love, which we owe Him for His benefits. It is most just, then, that we should imitate this conduct of God, in order, as the same St. Bernard says, that the grace should return to its Author by the same canal through which it came: *Ut eodem alveo ad largitorem gratiæ gratia redeat, quo fluxit,*—"That grace should return to the giver of grace by the same channel through which it came."

This is precisely what our devotion does. We offer and consecrate all we are and all we have to the Blessed Virgin, in order that our Lord may receive through her mediation the glory and the gratitude which we owe Him. We acknowledge ourselves unworthy and unfit to approach His Infinite Majesty by ourselves; and it is on this account that we avail ourselves of the intercession of the most holy Virgin.

Moreover, this devotion is a practice of great humility, which God loves above all the other virtues. A soul which exalts itself abases God; a soul which abases itself exalts God. God resists the proud, and gives His grace to the humble. If you abase yourself, thinking yourself unworthy to appear before Him and to draw nigh to Him, He descends, and lowers Himself to come to you, to take pleasure in you, and to exalt you in spite of yourself.

On the contrary, when you are hardy enough to approach God without a mediator, God flies from you, and you cannot reach Him. Oh, how He loves humility of heart! It is to this humility that our peculiar devotion engages us, because it teaches us never to draw nigh of ourselves to our Lord, however sweet and merciful He may be, but always to avail ourselves of the intercession of our Blessed Lady, whether it be to appear before God, or to speak to Him, or to draw near to Him, or to offer Him any thing, or to unite and consecrate ourselves to Him.

Third Motive

1. The most holy Virgin, who is a Mother of sweetness and mercy, and who never lets herself be vanquished in love and liberality, seeing that we give ourselves entirely to her, to honour and to serve her, and for that end strip ourselves of all that is dearest to us in order to adorn her, meets us in the same spirit. She also gives her whole self, and gives it in an unspeakable manner, to him who gives all to her. She causes him to be engulfed in the abyss of her graces. She adorns him with her merits; she supports him with her power; she illuminates him with her light; she inflames him with her love; she communicates to him her virtues, her humility, her faith, her purity, and the rest. She makes herself his bail, his supplement, and his dear all towards Jesus. In a word, as that person is all consecrated to Mary, so is Mary all for him; after such a fashion that we can say of that perfect servant and child of Mary what St. John the Evangelist said of himself, that he took the holy Virgin for all his goods,—*Accepit eam discipulus in sua,*—"The disciple took her for his own."

It is this which produces in the soul, if it is faithful, a great distrust, contempt, and hatred of self, and a great confidence and a great self-abandonment in the Blessed Virgin, its good Mistress. A man no longer, as before, leans on his own dispositions, intentions, merits, and good works; because, having made an entire sacrifice of them to Jesus Christ by that good Mother, he has but one treasure now, where all his goods are laid up, and that is no longer in himself; for his treasure is Mary. It is this which makes him approach our Lord without servile or scrupulous fear, and pray to Him with great confidence. It is this which makes him enter into the sentiments of the devout and learned Abbot Rupert, who, making an allusion to the victory that Jacob gained over the angel, said to our Blessed Lady these beautiful words: "O Mary, my Princess, Immaculate Mother of a God-man, Jesus Christ, I desire to wrestle with that Man, namely, the Divine Word, not armed with my own merits, but with yours." *O Domina, Dei Genitrix Maria, et incorrupta Mater Dei et Hominis, non meis, sed tuis armatus meritis, cum isto Viro, seu Verbo Dei, luctari cupio* (Rupert, *Prolog. in Cantic.*).

Oh, how strong and mighty we are with Jesus Christ, when we are armed with the worthy merits and intercession of the Mother of God, who, as St. Augustine says, has lovingly vanquished the Most High.

2. As by this practice we give to our Lord by His Mother's hands all our good works, that good Mother purifies them, embellishes them, and makes them acceptable to her Son.

1. She purifies them of all the soil of self-love, and of that imperceptible attachment to the creature, which slips incessantly into our best actions. As soon as they are in her most pure and fruitful hands, those same hands, which have never been sullied or idle, and which purify whatever they touch, take away from the present which we make to her all that was spoilt or imperfect about it.

2. She embellishes our works, in adorning them with her own merits and virtues. It is as if a peasant, wishing to gain the friendship and benevolence of the king, went to the queen, and presented her with a fruit, which was his whole revenue, in order that she might present it to the king. The queen, having accepted the poor little offering from the peasant, would place the fruit on a large and beautiful dish of gold, and so,

on the peasant's behalf, would present it to the king. Then the fruit, however unworthy in itself to be a king's present, would become worthy of his majesty, because of the dish of gold on which it rested and the person who presented it.

3. She presents these good works to Jesus Christ; for she keeps nothing of what is given for herself, as if she was our last end. She refers it all faithfully to Jesus. If we give to her, we give necessarily to Jesus; if we praise her or glorify her, we at once praise and glorify Jesus. As of old, when St. Elizabeth praised her, so now, when we praise and bless her, she sings herself, *Magnificat anima mea Dominum,*—"My soul doth magnify the Lord."

4. She persuades Jesus to accept these good works, however little and poor the present may be for that Saint of saints and that King of kings. When we present any thing to Jesus by ourselves, and relying on our own industry and disposition, Jesus examines the offering, and often rejects it because of the stains it has contracted through self-love; just as of old He rejected the sacrifices of the Jews when they were full of their own will. But when we present Him any thing by the pure and virginal hands of His Well-beloved, we take Him by His weak side, if it is allowable to use such a term. He does not consider so much the thing that is given Him, as the Mother who gives it. He does not consider so much whence the offering comes, as by whom it comes. Thus Mary, who is never repelled and always well received by her Son, makes every thing she presents to Him, great or small, acceptable to His Majesty. For Jesus to receive it and to take complacence in it, it is enough that Mary should present it. This is the great counsel which St. Bernard used to give to those whom he conducted to perfection: "When you want to offer any thing to God, take care to offer it by the most agreeable and worthy hands of Mary, unless you wish to have it rejected,"— *Modicum quod offerre desideras manibus Mariæ offerendum tradere cura, si non vis sustinere repulsam.*

Is not this what nature itself suggests to the little, with regard to the great, as we have already seen? Why should not grace lead us to do the same thing with regard to God, who is infinitely exalted above us, and before whom we are less than atoms? seeing, moreover, that we have an advocate so powerful that she is never refused; so full of inventions, that she knows all the secret ways of gaining the heart of God; and so good and charitable, that she repels no one, however little and wretched he may be.

I shall bring forward presently the true figure of these truths in the history of Jacob and Rebecca.

Fourth Motive

This devotion, faithfully practised, is an excellent means of making sure that the value of all our good works shall be employed for the greatest glory of God. Scarcely any one acts for that noble end, although we are all under an obligation to do so. Either we do not know where the greatest glory of God is to be found, or we do not wish to find it. But our Blessed Lady, to whom we cede the value and the merit of the good works we may do, knows most perfectly where the greatest glory of God is to be found; and, inasmuch as she never does any thing except for the greatest glory of God, a perfect servant of that good Mistress, who is wholly consecrated to her, may say with the hardiest assurance, that the value of all his actions, thoughts, and words, is employed for the greatest glory of God, at least unless he expressly revokes his offering. Is there any consolation equal to this, for a soul who loves God with a pure and disinterested love, and who prizes the glory and interests of God far beyond his own?

Fifth Motive

This devotion is an *easy*, *short*, *perfect*, and *secure* way of arriving at union with our Lord, in which the perfection of a Christian consists.

It is **an *easy* way.** It is the way which Jesus Christ Himself trod in coming to us, and in which there is no obstacle in arriving at Him. It is true that we can attain to divine union by other roads; but it is by many more crosses, and strange deaths, and with many more difficulties, which we shall find it hard to overcome. We must pass through obscure nights, through combats, through strange agonies, over craggy mountains, through cruel thorns, and over frightful deserts. But, by the path of Mary, we pass more gently and more tranquilly. We do find, it is true, great battles to fight, and great hardships to master; but that good Mother and Mistress makes herself so present and so near to her faithful servants, to enlighten them in their darknesses and their doubts, to strengthen them in their fears, and to sustain them in their struggles and their difficulties, that in truth this virginal path to find Jesus Christ is a path of roses and honey compared with the other paths. There have been some Saints, but they have been in small numbers, who have passed by this sweet path to go to Jesus, because the Holy Ghost, faithful Spouse of Mary, has by a singular grace disclosed it to them. Such were St. Ephrem, St. John Damascene, St. Bernard, St. Bernardine, St. Bonaventure, St. Francis of Sales, and others. But the rest of the Saints, who are the greater number, although they have all had devotion to our Blessed Lady, have not on that account, or at least very little, entered upon this way. This is why they have had to pass through ruder and more dangerous trials.

How comes it, then, some of the faithful servants of Mary will say to me, that the loyal clients of this good Mother have so many occasions of suffering, nay, even more than others who are not so devout to her? They are contradicted, they are persecuted, they are calumniated, the world cannot endure them; or, again, they walk in interior darknesses, and in deserts where there is not the least drop of the dew of heaven. If this devotion to our Blessed Lady makes the road to Jesus easier, how comes it that they who follow it are the most despised of men? I reply, that it is quite true that the most faithful servants of the Blessed Virgin, being also her greatest favourites, receive from her the greatest graces and favours of heaven, which are crosses. But I maintain that it is also the servants of Mary who carry these crosses with more facility, more merit, and more glory. That which would stay the progress of another a thousand times over, or perhaps would make him fall, does not once arrest their steps, but rather enables them to advance; because that good Mother, all full of the graces and unction of the Holy Ghost, preserves all the crosses, which she cuts for them, in the sugar of her maternal sweetness, so that they swallow them gaily, like preserved fruits, however bitter they may be in themselves; and I believe that a person who wishes to be devout, and to live piously in Jesus Christ, and consequently to suffer persecutions, and carry his cross daily, will never carry great crosses, or carry them joyously or perseveringly, without a tender devotion to our Lady, which is the sweetmeat and confection of crosses; just as a person would not be able to eat unripe fruits, without a great effort which he could hardly keep up, unless they had been preserved in sugar.

This devotion to the Blessed Virgin is **a *short* road** to find Jesus Christ, both because it is a road which we do not stray from, and because, as I have just said, it is a road we tread with joy and facility, and by consequence with promptitude. We make more progress in a brief period of submission to, and dependence on, Mary than in whole years of our own will, and of resting upon ourselves. A man obedient and submissive to Mary shall sing the signal victories which he shall gain over his enemies. They will try to hinder his advancing, or to make him retrace his steps, or to fall. This is true. But with the support, the aid, and the guidance of Mary, without falling, without drawing back one step, without even slackening his pace, he shall advance with giant strides towards Jesus, along the same path by which he knows that Jesus also came to us with giant strides, and in the briefest space of time. Why do you think that Jesus lived so short a time on earth, and of those few years spent nearly all of them in subjection and obedience to His Mother? Ah, this is the truth: that He was perfected indeed in a short time, but that He lived a long time, longer than Adam, whose fall He had come to repair, although the patriarch lived above nine hundred years. Jesus Christ lived a long time, because He lived in complete subjection to His holy Mother, and closely united with her, in order that He might thus obey God His Father. For the Holy Ghost says that a man who honours his mother is like a man who layeth up a treasure; that is to say, he who honours Mary his Mother, up to the point of subjecting himself to her and obeying her in all things, will soon become exceedingly rich, (1) because he is every day amassing treasures, by the secret of that philosopher's-stone,—*Qui honorat matrem quasi qui thesaurizat,*—"He who honours his mother is as one who lays up a treasure;" (2) because it is the bosom of Mary which has surrounded and engendered a perfect man, and has had the capacity of containing Him whom the whole universe could neither contain nor comprehend,—it is, I say, in the bosom of Mary that they who are youthful become elders in light, in holiness, in experience, and in wisdom; and that we arrive in a few years at the fulness of the age of Jesus Christ.

> *The Most High... has come to us by her, without losing any thing of His divinity and sanctity.*

This practice of devotion to our Blessed Lady is also **a *perfect* path** by which to go and unite ourselves to Jesus, because the divine Mary is the most perfect and the most holy of creatures, and because Jesus, who has come to us most perfectly, took no other road for His great and admirable journey. The Most High, the Incomprehensible, the Inaccessible, He Who Is, has deigned to come to us, little worms of earth who are nothing. How has He done this? The Most High has come down to us perfectly and divinely by the humble Mary. He has come to us by her, without losing any thing of His divinity and sanctity. So it is by Mary that the unspeakably little are to ascend, perfectly and divinely, without any fear, to the Most High. The Incomprehensible has allowed Himself to be comprehended and perfectly contained by the little Mary, without losing any thing of His immensity. So also it is by the little Mary that we must let ourselves be held and guided perfectly without any reserve. The Inaccessible has drawn near to us, and has closely united Himself to us, perfectly, and even personally, to our humanity, by Mary, without losing any of His Majesty. So also is it by Mary that we must draw near to God, and unite ourselves perfectly and closely to His Majesty, without fear of being repulsed. In a word, He Who Is has designed to come to that which is not, and to make that which is not become God in Him Who Is; and He has done this perfectly in giving Himself and subjecting Himself entirely to the young Virgin Mary without ceasing to be in time He who is eternal. In like manner it is by Mary that we, who are nothing, can become like to God by grace and glory, by giving ourselves to her so perfectly and entirely as to be nothing in ourselves but every thing in her, without fear of delusion.

Make for me, if you will, a new road to go to Jesus, and pave it with all the merits of the Blessed, adorn it with all their heroic virtues, illuminate and embellish it with all the lights and beauties of the Angels, and let all the Angels and Saints be there themselves to escort, defend, and sustain those who are ready to walk there; and yet in truth, in simple truth, I say boldly, and I repeat that I say truly, I would prefer to this new perfect path the immaculate way of Mary. P*osui immaculatam viam meam.* It is the way without any stain or spot, without original or actual sin, without shadow or darkness. When my sweet Jesus in His glory comes a second time on earth, as it is most certain He will do, to reign there, He will choose no other way for His journey than the divine Mary, by whom He came the first time so surely and so perfectly. But there will be a difference between His first and His last coming. The first time He came secretly and hiddenly; the second time He will come gloriously and resplendently. But both times He will come perfectly, because both times He will come by Mary. Alas, here is a mystery which is not understood. *Hic taceat omnis lingua,*—"Here let all tongues be mute."

This devotion to our Blessed Lady is also **a *secure* way** to go to Jesus, and to acquire perfection by uniting us to Him.

1. It is a secure way, because the practice which I am teaching is not new. M. Boudon, who died a little while ago in the odour of sanctity, says, in a book which he composed on this devotion, that it is so ancient we cannot fix precisely the date of its commencement. It is, however, certain that for more than seven hundred years we find traces of it in the Church. St. Odilon, the abbot of Cluny, who lived about the year 1040, was one of the first who publicly practised it in France; as is remarked in his life. Cardinal Peter Damien relates that, in the year 1036, the Blessed Marino, his brother, made himself a slave of the Blessed Virgin in the presence of his director, in a most edifying manner. He put a rope round his neck, took the discipline, and laid on the altar a sum of money, to mark his devotion and consecration to our Lady; and he continued this devotion so faithfully during his whole life, that he deserved to be visited and consoled at his death by his good Mistress, and to receive from her mouth the promise of Paradise in recompense for his services.

Cesarius Bollandus mentions an illustrious cavalier, Vautier de Birbac, who, about the year 1500, consecrated himself to the Blessed Virgin. This devotion was also practised by several private persons up to the seventeenth century, when it became public.

Father Simon de Roxas, of the Order of the Redemption of Captives, and preacher of Philip the Third, made this devotion popular in Spain and Germany; and through the instance of Philip the Third, he obtained of Gregory the Fifteenth ample indulgences for those who practised it. Father de Los Rios, the Augustinian, devoted himself, with his intimate friend, Father Roxas, to spread this devotion, both by preaching and writing, through Spain and Germany. He composed a thick volume, called *Hierarchia Mariana*, in which he treats, with as much piety as learning, of the antiquity, excellence, and solidity of this devotion. The Theatine Fathers, in the seventeenth century, established this devotion in Italy, Sicily, and Savoy. Father Stanislas Phalacius, the Jesuit, increased this devotion wonderfully in Poland. Father de Los Rios, in his work just cited, quotes the names of princes, princesses, dukes, and cardinals, of different kingdoms, who embraced this devotion.

Cornelius à Lapide, as much recommended for his piety as for his profound erudition, having received a commission from several theologians to examine this devotion, did so with great maturity and deliberation, and praised it in a manner which we might have expected from his well-known piety; and many other distinguished persons have followed his example.

The Jesuit Fathers, always zealous in the service of our Blessed Lady, presented, in the name of the Congreganists of Cologne, a little treatise on this devotion to the Duke Ferdinand of Bavaria, who was then Archbishop of Cologne. He gave it his approbation, and permission to print it; and exhorted all the parish-priests and religious of his diocese to promote the devotion as much as ever they could. Cardinal Berulle, whose memory is in benediction through all France, was one of the most zealous in spreading this devotion in that country, in spite of all the calumnies and persecutions which he suffered from critics and libertines. They accused him of novelty and superstition. They wrote and published against him, a libel in order to defame him; and they made use, or rather it was the devil by their ministry, of a thousand subtleties to hinder his spreading the devotion in France. But that great and holy man only answered their calumnies by his patience; and he met the objections contained in their libel by a short treatise, in which he most convincingly refuted them. He showed them that the devotion was founded on the example of Jesus Christ, on the obligations which we have to Him, and on the vows which we have made in holy Baptism. It was chiefly by this last reason that he shut his adversaries' mouths, making them see that this consecration to the holy Virgin, and to Jesus Christ by her hands, is nothing else than a perfect renewal of the vows and promises of Baptism. He has said many beautiful things on this practice, which can be read in his works.

We may also see in M. Boudon's book the different Popes who have approved this devotion, the theologians who have examined it, the persecutions they have undergone and have overcome, and the thousands of persons who have embraced it, without any Pope having ever condemned it. Indeed, we cannot see how it could be condemned without overturning the foundations of Christianity. It is clear, then, that this devotion is not new; and that if it is not common, it is because it is too precious to be relished and practised by all the world.[1]

2. This devotion is a secure means of going to Jesus Christ, because it is the very characteristic of our Blessed Lady to conduct us surely to Jesus, just as it is the very characteristic of Jesus to conduct us surely to the Eternal Father. Spiritual persons, therefore, must not fall into the false belief that Mary can be a hindrance to them attaining to divine union; for is it possible that she who has found grace before God for the whole world in general,

---

1. Boudon says, in his *Saint Esclavage*, that the English Catholics were remarkable for this devotion in the seventeenth century. – F.W.F.

and for each one in particular, should be a hindrance to a soul in finding the great grace of union with Him? Can it be possible that she who has been all full and superabounding with graces, so united and transformed into God that it has been a kind of necessity that He should be incarnate in her, should be a stumbling-block in the way of a soul's perfect union with God? It is quite true that the view of other creatures, however holy, may perhaps at certain times retard divine union. But this cannot be said of Mary, as I have remarked before, and shall never weary of repeating. One reason why so few souls come to the fulness of the age of Jesus Christ is because Mary, who is as much as ever the Mother of the Son, and as much as ever the fruitful Spouse of the Holy Ghost, is not sufficiently formed in their hearts. He who wishes to have the fruit well ripened and well formed must have the tree that produces it; he who wishes to have the fruit of life, Jesus Christ, must have the tree of life, which is Mary; he who wishes to have in himself the operation of the Holy Ghost must have His faithful and indissoluble Spouse, the divine Mary, who makes Him fertile and fruit-bearing, as we have said elsewhere.

...it is the very characteristic of our Blessed Lady to conduct us surely to Jesus, just as it is the very characteristic of Jesus to conduct us surely to the Eternal Father.

Be persuaded, then, that the more you look at Mary in your prayers, contemplations, actions, and sufferings, if not with a distinct and definite view, at least with a general and imperceptible one, the more perfectly you will find Jesus Christ, who is always with Mary, great, powerful, operative, and incomprehensible.

Thus, so far from the divine Mary, all absorbed in God, being an obstacle to the perfect in their attaining to union with God, there has never been up to this point, and there never will be, any creature who will aid us more efficaciously in this great work, whether by the graces she will communicate to us for this effect,—for, as a Saint has said, no one can be filled with the thought of God except by her, *Nemo cogitatione Dei repletur, nisi per te,*—or whether by freedom from the illusions and trickeries of the evil spirit, which she will guarantee to us.

Where Mary is, there the evil spirit is not. One of the most infallible marks

we can have of our being conducted by the good Spirit is our being very devout to Mary, our thinking often of her, and our speaking often of her.

This last is the thought of a Saint, who adds, that as respiration is a certain sign the body is not dead, the frequent thought and loving invocation
of Mary is a certain sign the soul is not dead by sin.

As it is Mary alone, says the Church (and the Holy Ghost, who guides the
Church), who alone makes all heresies come to naught (*Sola cunctas hæreses
interemisti in universo mundo*,—"Thou alone hast destroyed all heresies in
the whole world"), we may be sure that, however critics may grumble, no
faithful client of Mary will ever fall into heresy or illusion, at least formal. He
may very well err materially, take falsehood for truth, and the evil spirit for
the good; and yet he will do even this with more difficulty than others. But
sooner or later he will acknowledge his material fault and error; and when
he knows it, he will not be in any way self-opinionated in believing and main-
taining what he had once thought true. Whoever, then, wishes to put aside
the fear of illusion, which is the besetting timidity of men of prayer, and to
advance in the way of perfection, and surely and perfectly to find Jesus Christ,
let him embrace with great-heartedness (*corde magno et animo volenti*,—
"with a great heart and a willing mind") this devotion to our Blessed Lady,
which perhaps he has not known before; let him enter into this excellent
way, which was unknown to him, and which I now point out: *Excellentiorem
viam vobis demonstro*,—"I show you a more excellent way."

It is a path trodden by Jesus Christ, the Incarnate Wisdom, our sole Head.
One of His members in passing by the same road cannot deceive himself.
It is an *easy* road, because of the fulness of the grace and unction of the Holy
Ghost, which fills it to overflowing. No one wearies there; no one walking
there has ever to retrace his steps. It is a *short* road, which leads us to Jesus
in a little time. It is a *perfect* road, where there is no mud, no dust, nor the
least spot of sin. Lastly, it is a *secure* road, which conducts us to Jesus Christ
and life eternal in a straight and secure manner, without turning to the right
hand or to the left. Let us, then, set forth upon that road, and walk there
day and night, until we come to the fulness of the age of Jesus Christ.

Sixth Motive

This practice of devotion gives to those who make use of it faithfully a great
interior liberty, which is the liberty of the children of God. For, as by this
devotion we make ourselves slaves of Jesus Christ, and consecrate our-

selves entirely to Him in this capacity, our Good Master, in recompense for the loving captivity in which we put ourselves, (a) takes all scruple and servile fear from the soul, with every thing that is capable of contracting, imprisoning, or confusing it; (b) He enlarges the heart by a firm confidence in God, making it look at Him as a Father; and (c) He inspires us with a tender and filial love.

Without stopping to prove these truths by arguments, I shall be content to quote here what I have read in the life of Mother Agnes of Jesus, a Dominicaness of the convent of Langeac, in Auvergne; who died there, in the odour of sanctity, in the year 1634. When she was only seven years old, and was suffering from great spiritual pains, she heard a voice which told her that if she wished to be delivered from all her pains, and to be protected against all her enemies, she was as quickly as possible to make herself the slave of Jesus and His most holy Mother. She had no sooner returned to the house than she gave herself up entirely to Jesus and His Mother in this capacity, although up to that time she had not known so much as what the devotion meant. Having found an iron chain, she put it round her body, and wore it to her death. After this action, all her pains and scruples ceased, and she found herself in a great peace and dilatation of heart. It was this which engaged her to teach the devotion to many persons, who made great progress in it, and, among others, to M. Olier, the founder of St. Sulpice, and to many priests and ecclesiastics of the same seminary. One day our Lady appeared to her, and put round her neck a chain of gold, to testify the joy she had in Mother Agnes having made herself her Son's slave and her own; and St. Cecilia, who accompanied our Lady in that apparition, said to the religious: "Happy are the faithful slaves of the Queen of Heaven; for they shall enjoy true liberty,"—*Tibi servire libertas.*

Seventh Motive

Another consideration which may engage us to embrace this practice is that of the great good which our neighbour will receive from it. For by this practice we exercise charity towards him in an eminent manner, seeing that we give him by Mary's hands all that is most precious to ourselves,— which is the satisfactory and impetratory value of all our good works, without excepting the least good thought, or the least little suffering. We agree that all the satisfactions we may have acquired, or may acquire up to the moment of our death, should be employed at our Lady's will, either for the conversion of sinners, or for the deliverance of souls from Purgatory.

Is not this to love our neighbour perfectly? Is not this to be the true disciple of Jesus Christ, who is always to be recognised by his charity? Is not this the way to convert sinners without any fear of vanity; and to deliver souls from Purgatory, without scarcely doing any thing but what we are obliged to do by our state of life?

To understand the excellence of this motive, we must understand also what a good it is to convert a sinner, or to deliver a soul from Purgatory. It is an infinite good, which is greater than to create heaven and earth, because we give to a soul the possession of God. If by this practice we deliver but one soul in our life from Purgatory, or convert but one sinner, would not that be enough to induce a truly charitable man to embrace it? But we must remark that, inasmuch as our good works pass through the hands of Mary, they receive an augmentation of purity, and consequently of merit, and of satisfactory and impetratory value. On this account they become more capable of solacing the souls in Purgatory and of converting sinners than if they did not pass by the virginal and liberal hands of Mary. It may be little that we give by our Lady; but, in truth, if it is given without our own will, and with a disinterested charity, that little becomes very mighty to turn the wrath of God, and to attract His mercy. It would be no wonder if, at the hour of death, it should be found that a person faithful to this practice shall, by the means of it, have delivered many souls from Purgatory, and converted many sinners, though he shall have done nothing more than the ordinary actions of his state of life. What joy at his judgment! What glory in his eternity!

Eighth Motive

Lastly, that which in some sense most persuasively engages us to this devotion to our Lady is, that it is an admirable means of persevering and being faithful in virtue. Whence comes it that the majority of the conversions of sinners are not durable? Whence comes it that we relapse so easily into sin? Whence comes it that the greater part of the just, instead of advancing from virtue to virtue and acquiring new graces, often lose the little virtue and the little grace they have? This misfortune comes, as I have shown before, from the fact that man is at once so corrupt, so feeble, and so inconstant, and yet trusts to himself, leans on his own strength, and believes himself capable of guarding the treasure of his graces, of his virtues and merits. On the other hand, by this devotion we confide all we possess to the Blessed Virgin, who is faithful; we take her for the universal depositary of all our goods of nature and of grace. It is to her fidelity that we trust them. It is on her power that we lean. It is on her mercy and charity that we build, in order that she may preserve and augment our virtues and merits, in spite of the devil, the world, and the flesh, who put forth all their efforts to take them from us. We say to her, as a good child to his mother, and a faithful servant to her mistress, *Depositum custodi*,—"My good Mother and Mistress, I acknowledge that up to this time I have, by your intercession, received more grace from God than I deserve; and my sad experience teaches me that I carry this treasure in a very frail vessel, and that I am too weak and too miserable to keep it safely of myself. I beseech you, therefore, receive in trust all which I possess,

> *"When Mary holds you up, you will not fall; when she protects you, you need not fear; when she leads you, you will not tire yourself; when she is favourable to you, you will arrive at the harbour of safety."* —St. Bernard

and keep it for me by your fidelity and power. If you keep it for me, I shall lose nothing; if you hold me up, I shall not fall; if you protect me, I shall be sheltered from my enemies." Listen to what St. Bernard said in former times, in order to encourage us to adopt this practice: "When Mary holds you up, you will not fall; when she protects you, you need not fear; when she leads you, you will not tire yourself; when she is favourable to you, you will arrive at the harbour of safety,"—*Ipsa tenente, non corruis; ipsa propitia, pervenis.* St. Bonaventure seems to say the same thing in still more formal terms. "The Blessed Virgin," he says, "is not only retained in the plenitude of the Saints, but she also retains and keeps the Saints in their plenitude, so that it may not diminish. She hinders their virtues from being dissipated, their merits from withering, their graces from being lost, the devils from hurting them, and even our Lord from punishing them when they sin." *Virgo non solum in plenitudine sanctorum detinetur, sed etiam in plenitudine sanctos detinet, ne plenitudo minuatur; detinet virtutes, ne fugiant; detinet merita, ne pereant; detinet gratias, ne effluant; detinet dæmones, ne noceant; detinet Filium, ne peccatores percutiat* (St. Bonaventure, In Specul. B.V.).

Our Blessed Lady is the faithful Virgin, who by her fidelity to God repairs the losses which the faithless Eve has caused by her infidelity. It is she who obtains the graces of fidelity and perseverance for those who attach themselves to her. It is on this account that a Saint compares her to a firm anchor, which holds them fast, and hinders their making shipwreck in the agitated sea of this world, where so many persons perish simply through not being fastened to that anchor. "We fasten our souls," says he, "to thy hope, as to an abiding anchor,"—*Animas ad spem tuam sicut ad firmam ancoram alligamus.* It is to her that the Saints who have saved themselves have been the most attached, and have done their best to attach others, in order to persevere in virtue. Happy then, a thousand times happy, are the Christians who are now fastened faithfully and entirely to her, as to a firm anchor! The violence of the storms of this world will not make them founder, nor sink their heavenly treasures. Happy those who enter into Mary, as into the ark of Noe! The waters of the deluge of sin, which drowns so great a portion of the world, shall do no harm to them. *Qui operantur in me non peccabunt,*—"They who work in me shall not sin," says Mary, with the Divine Wisdom. Blessed are the faithless children of the unhappy Eve, if only they attach themselves to the faithful Mother and Virgin, who remains always faithful, and never belies herself,—*Fidelis permanet; seipsam negare non potest*! She always loves those who love her,—*Ego diligentes me diligo,*—not only with an affective love, but with an effectual and efficacious one, by hindering them, through a great abundance of graces, from drawing back in the pursuit of virtue, from falling in the road, and from losing the grace of her Son. This good Mother, always out of pure charity, receives whatever we deposit with her; and what she has once received in her office of depositary, she is obliged by justice, in virtue of the contract of trusteeship, to keep safely for us: just as a person, with whom I have left a thousand pounds in trust, would be under the obligation of keeping them safely for me; so that if, by his negligence, they were lost, he would in justice be responsible to me for them. But the faithful Mary cannot let any thing which has been intrusted to her be lost through her negligence. Heaven and earth could pass away sooner than she could be negligent or faithless to those who trust in her.

Poor children of Mary, your weakness is extreme, your inconstancy is great, your inward nature is thoroughly corrupted, you are drawn (I grant it) from the same corrupt mass as all the children of Adam and Eve. Yet do not be discouraged on that account. Console yourselves, and exult in having the secret which I teach you,—a secret unknown to almost all Christians, even the most devout. Leave not your gold and silver in your coffers, which have been already broken open by the evil spirits, who have robbed you. Those coffers are too little, too weak, too old, to hold a treasure so precious and so great. Put not the pure and clear water of the fountain into your vessels, all spoilt and infected by sin. If the sin is there no longer, at least the odour of it is, and so the water will be spoilt. Put not your exquisite wines into your old casks, which have had bad wine in them; else even these wines will be spoilt, and perhaps break the casks, and be spilled upon the ground.

Though you, predestinate souls, understand me well enough, I will speak yet more openly. Trust not the gold of your charity, the silver of your purity, the waters of your heavenly graces, nor the wines of your merits and virtues, to a torn sack, an old and broken coffer, a spoilt and corrupted vessel, like yourselves; else you will be stripped by the robbers,—that is to say, the demons,—who are seeking and watching night and day for the right time to do it; and you will infect, by your own bad odour of self-love, self-confidence, and self-will, every most pure thing which God has given you. Pour, pour into the bosom and heart of Mary all your treasures, all your graces, all your virtues. She is a spiritual vessel, she is a vessel of honour, she is a marvellous vessel of devotion,—*Vas spirituale, vas honorabile, vas insigne devotionis.*

'ALL THAT I HAVE IS THINE, AND ALL THAT THOU HAST IS MINE.'

Since God Himself has been shut up in person, with all His perfections, in that vessel, it has become altogether spiritual, and the spiritual abode of the most spiritual souls. It has become honourable, and the throne of honour for the grandest princes of eternity. It has become wonderful in devotion, and a dwelling the most illustrious for sweetnesses, for graces, and for virtues. It has become rich as a house of gold, strong as a tower of David, and pure as a tower of victory. Oh! how happy is the man who has given every thing to Mary, and has trusted himself to Mary in every thing and for every thing! He belongs all to Mary and Mary belongs all to him. He can say boldly with David, *Hæc facta est mihi,*—"Mary is made for me;" or with the beloved disciple, *Accepi eam in mea,*—"I have taken her for all my goods;" or with Jesus Christ, *Omnia mea tua sunt, et omnia tua mea sunt,*—"All that I have is thine, and all that thou hast is mine."

If any critic who reads this shall take it into his head that I speak here exaggeratedly, and with an extravagance of devotion, alas! he does not understand me, either because he is a carnal man, who has no relish for spiritual things; or because he is a worldling, who cannot receive the Holy Ghost; or because he is proud and critical, condemning and despising whatever he does not understand himself. But the souls which are not born of blood, nor of flesh, nor of the will of man, but of God and Mary, understand me and relish me; and it is for these that I write. Nevertheless, I say now both for the one and for the other, in returning from this digression, that the divine Mary, being the most gracious and liberal of all pure creatures, never lets herself be overcome in love and liberality. As a holy man said of her, for an egg, she gives an ox; that is to say, for a little that is given to her, she gives much of what she has received from God. Hence, if a soul gives itself to her without reserve, she gives herself to that soul without reserve, if only we put our confidence in her without presumption, and labour on our side to acquire virtues, and to bridle our passions.

Let, then, the faithful servants of the Blessed Virgin say hardily with St. John Damascene, "Having confidence in you, O Mother of God, I shall be saved; being under your protection, I shall fear nothing; with your succour, I shall give battle to my enemies, and put them to flight; for devotion to you is an arm of salvation, which God gives to those whom it is His will to save." *Spem tuam habens, O Deipara, servabor; defensionem tuam possidens, non timebo; persequar inimicos meos et in fugam vertam, habens protectionem et auxilium tuum; nam tibi devotum esse est arma quædam salutis quæ Deus his dat quos vult salvos fieri* (St. John Damascene).

CHAPTER 8

Figure of this Consecration in the History of Jacob Receiving the Blessing of Isaac through the Offices of Rebecca

O f all the truths which I have been putting forward with regard to our Blessed Lady and her children and servants, the Holy Ghost gives us an admirable figure in the Scriptures. It is in the history of Jacob, who received the benediction of his father Isaac, by the skill and pains of Rebecca, his mother. This is the history, as the Holy Ghost relates it. I will afterwards add the explanation of it.

Esau having sold Jacob his birthright, Rebecca, the mother of the two brothers, who loved Jacob tenderly, secured this advantage to him many years afterwards by an address most holy but most full of mystery. Isaac, feeling himself very old and wishing to bless his children before he died, called his son Esau, who was his favourite, and commanded him to go out hunting, to get him something to eat, in order that he might bless him afterwards. Rebecca promptly informed Jacob of what had passed, and ordered him to go and take two kids from the flock. When he had given them to his mother, she prepared for Isaac what she knew he liked. She clothed Jacob in the garments of Esau, which she kept, and covered his hands and his neck with the skin of the kids, so that his father, who was blind, might, in hearing Jacob's voice, think at least by the skin of his hands that it was Esau his brother. Isaac, having been surprised by the voice, which he thought was Jacob's voice, made him come near him. Having touched the skins with which his hands were covered, he said that the voice truly was the voice of Jacob, but that the hands were the hands of Esau. After he had eaten, and, in kissing Jacob, had smelt the odour of his perfumed garments, he blessed him, and wished for him the dew of heaven and the fruitfulness of earth. He made him lord over all his brethren, and finished his blessing with these words, "Cursed be he that curseth thee, and let him that blesseth thee be filled with blessings." Isaac had hardly finished these words when Esau entered, and brought with him what he had captured while out hunting, in order that his father might eat it, and then bless him. The holy patriarch was surprised with an incredible astonishment when he understood what had happened. But, far from retracting what he had done, on the contrary he confirmed it, for he saw too plainly that the finger of God was in the matter. Esau then uttered great cries, as the holy Scripture remarks, and loudly accusing the deceitfulness of his brother, he asked his father if he had but one benediction; being in this point, as the holy Fathers remark, the image of those who are too glad to ally God with the world, and are fain to enjoy the consolations of heaven and the consolations of earth both together. At last Isaac, touched with the cries of Esau, blessed him, but with a blessing of the earth, subjecting him to his brother. This made him conceive such an envenomed hatred to Jacob, that he waited only for his father's death, in order to kill him. Neither would Jacob have escaped death, if his dear mother Rebecca had not saved him from it by her industries, and by the good counsels which she gave him, and which he followed.

Before explaining this beautiful history, we must observe that, according to the holy Fathers and the interpreters of Scripture, Jacob is the figure of Jesus Christ and the predestinate, and Esau that of the reprobate. We have but got to examine the actions and conduct of the one and the other to form our judgment about this.

Esau – The Figure of the Reprobate

1. Esau, the elder, was strong and robust of body, adroit and skilful in drawing the bow, and in taking much game in the chase. 2. He hardly ever stayed in the house; and putting no confidence in any thing but his own strength and address, he only worked out of doors. 3. He took very little pains to please his mother Rebecca, and indeed did nothing for that end. 4. He was such a glutton, and loved eating so much, that he sold his birthright for a mess of pottage. 5. He was, like Cain, full of envy against his brother Jacob, and persecuted him beyond measure.

Now this is the daily conduct of the reprobate. 1. They trust in their own strength and aptitude for temporal affairs. They are very strong, very able, and very enlightened in earthly business; but very weak and very ignorant in heavenly things,—*In terrenis fortes, in cœlestibus debiles.* 2. It is on this account that they are hardly at all, or at least very little, at their own homes,—that is to say, in their own interior, which is the inward and essential house which God has given to every man, to live there after His example; for God always rests in Himself. The reprobate do not love retirement, nor spirituality, nor inward devotion; and they treat as little, or as bigots, or as savages, those who are interior or retired from the world, and who work more within than without. 3. The reprobate care next to nothing for devotion to our Blessed Lady, the Mother of the predestinate. It is true that they do not hate her formally. Indeed, they sometimes praise her, and say they love her, and even practise some devotion in her honour. Nevertheless they cannot bear that we should love her tenderly, because they have not the tendernesses of Jacob for her. They find much to say against the practices of devotion, in which her good children and servants faithfully employ themselves in order to gain her affection, because they do not think that devotion necessary to salvation; and they consider, that provided they do not hate our Lady formally, or openly despise her devotion, it is enough. Moreover, they imagine that they are already in her good graces, and that, in fine, they are her servants, inasmuch as they recite and mumble certain prayers in her honour, without tenderness for her, or amendment in themselves. 4. The reprobate sell their birthright; that is to say, the pleasures of paradise. They sell it for a pottage of lentils; that is to say, for the pleasures of the earth. They laugh, they drink, they eat, they amuse themselves, they gamble, they dance, and take no more pains than Esau did to render themselves worthy of the benediction of their heavenly Father. In a word, they think only of earth, and they love earth only; and they speak and act only for earth and for its pleasures, selling for one moment of enjoyment, for one vain puff of honour, and for a morsel of hard metal, yellow or white, their baptismal grace, their robe of innocence, and their heavenly inheritance. 5. Finally, the reprobate daily hate and persecute the predestinate openly and secretly. They feel the predestinate as a burden to them, they despise them, they criticise them, they counterwork them, they abuse them, they rob them, they cheat them, they impoverish them, they drive them away, they bring them low into the dust; while they themselves are making fortunes, are taking their pleasures, getting themselves into good positions, enriching themselves, aggrandising themselves, and living at their ease.

Jacob – The Figure of Jesus Christ and the Predestinate

As to Jacob, the younger: 1. He was of a feeble constitution, meek and peaceful. He lived for the most part at home, in order to gain the good graces of his mother Rebecca, whom he loved tenderly. If he went abroad, it was not of his own will, nor through any confidence in his own industry, but to obey his mother.

2. He loved and honoured his mother. It was on this account that he kept at home. He avoided every thing which could displease her, and did every thing which he thought would please her; and this increased the love which Rebecca already had for him.

3. He was subject in all things to his dear mother. He obeyed her entirely in all matters,—promptly, without delaying, and lovingly, without complaining. At the least token of her will, the little Jacob ran and worked; and he believed every thing she said to him. For example: when she told him to fetch two kids, and that he should fetch them in order that she should prepare something for his father Isaac to eat, Jacob did not reply that one was enough to make a dish for a single man, but without reasoning he did what she told him to do.

4. He had a great confidence in his dear mother. As he did not lean in the least on his own ability, he leant exclusively on the care and protection of his mother. He appealed to her in all his necessities, and consulted her in all his doubts. For example: when he asked if instead of a blessing, he should not receive a curse from his father, he believed her and trusted her, when she said that she would take the curse upon herself.

5. Lastly, he imitated as far as he could the virtues he saw in his mother. It seems as if one of his reasons for leading such a sedentary life at home was to imitate his dear mother, who was virtuous, and kept herself removed from bad companies, which corrupt the morals. By this means he made himself worthy to receive the double benediction of his beloved father.

Such also is the conduct which the predestinate daily observe.

1. They are sedentary, and home-keepers, with their Mother. In other words, they love retirement, and are interior. They give themselves to prayer; but it is after the example and in the company of their Mother the holy Virgin, the whole of whose glory is within, and who, during her whole life, so much loved retirement and prayer. It is true that they sometimes appear without, in the world; but it is in obedience to the will of God, and that of their dear Mother, to fulfil the duties of their state. However apparently important their outward works may be, they esteem still more highly those which they do within themselves, in their interior, in the company of the Blessed Virgin. For it is within that they accomplish the great work of their perfection, compared with which all their other works are but infant sports. It is on this account that, while sometimes their brothers and sisters are working outwardly with much energy, success, and skill, in the

praise and with the approbation of the world, they, on the contrary, know by the light of the Holy Ghost that there is far more glory, more good, and more pleasure, in remaining hidden in retreat with Jesus Christ their Model, in an entire and perfect subjection to their Mother, than to do of themselves wonders of nature and grace in the world, as so many Esaus and reprobates do. *Gloria et divitiæ in domo ejus,*—"Glory for God, and riches for men are to be found in the house of Mary."

Lord Jesus, how sweet are Thy tabernacles! The sparrow has found a house to lodge in, and the turtle-dove a nest for her little ones. Oh, happy is the man who dwells in the house of Mary, where Thou wert the first to make Thy dwelling! It is in this house of the predestinate that he receives succour from Thee alone, and that he has disposed the steps and ascents of all the virtues, to raise himself in his heart to perfection in this vale of tears. *Quam dilecta tabernacula tua!*—"How lovely are Thy tabernacles!"

Oh, happy is the man who dwells in the house of Mary, where Thou wert the first to make Thy dwelling!

2. The predestinate tenderly love and truly honour our Blessed Lady as their good Mother and Mistress. They love her not only by mouth, but in truth. They honour her not only outwardly, but in the bottom of their hearts. They avoid, like Jacob, every thing which can displease her; and they practise with fervour whatever they think will make them find favour with her. They bring to her, and give her, not two kids, as Jacob did to Rebecca, but their body and their soul, with all that depends on them, figured by the two kids of Jacob. They bring them to her, (a) that she may receive them as things which belong to her; (b) that she may kill them, and make them die to sin and self, in stripping them of their own skin, and their own self-love, and by this means to please Jesus her Son, who wills not to have any for His disciples and friends but those who are dead to themselves; (c) that she may prepare them for the taste of our Heavenly Father, and for His greatest glory, which she knows better than any other creature; and (d) that by her cares and intercessions this body and soul, thoroughly purified from every stain, thoroughly dead, thoroughly stripped, and well prepared, may be a delicate meat, worthy of the mouth and the blessing of our Heavenly Father. Is not this what the predestinate do, who relish and practise the per-

fect consecration to Jesus Christ by the hands of Mary, which we are now teaching them, by way of testifying to Jesus and Mary an effective and courageous love?

The reprobate tell us loudly enough that they love Jesus, and that they love and honour Mary; but it is not with their substance, it is not up to the point of sacrificing to them their body with its senses, their soul with its passions, as the predestinate do. These last are subject and obedient to our Blessed Lady, as to their good Mother; after the example of Jesus Christ, who, of the three-and-thirty years He lived on earth, employed thirty to glorify God His Father, by a perfect and entire subjection to His holy Mother.

3. The predestinate obey Mary in following exactly her counsels, as the little Jacob did those of Rebecca, who said to him, *Acquiesce consiliis meis,*—"My son, follow my counsels;" or like the people at the marriage of Cana, to whom our Lady said, *Quodcumque dixerit vobis, facite,*—"Whatever my Son shall say to you, that do." Jacob, for having obeyed his mother, received the blessing, as it were, miraculously, although naturally he would not have had it. The people at the marriage of Cana, for having followed our Lady's counsel, were honoured with our Lord's first miracle, who there changed the water into wine at the prayer of His holy Mother. In like manner, all those who, to the end of time, shall receive the benediction of our Heavenly Father, and shall be honoured by the wonders of God, shall only receive their graces in consequence of their perfect obedience to Mary. The Esaus, on the contrary, lose their blessing through their want of subjection to the Blessed Virgin.

4. The predestinate have also a great confidence in the goodness and power of our Blessed Lady, their good Mother. They call incessantly for her help. They look upon her as their polar star, to lead them to a good port. They lay bare to her their pains and their necessities with much openness of heart. They attach themselves to her mercy and her sweetness, in order to get the pardon of their sins by her intercession, or to taste her maternal sweetnesses in their pains and wearinesses.

They even throw themselves, hide themselves, and lose themselves in an admirable manner in her loving and virginal bosom, that they may be set on fire there of pure love, that they may be cleansed there from their least stain, and fully to find Jesus, who dwells there, as on His most glorious throne. O what happiness! "Think not," says the Abbot Gueric, "that it is happier to dwell in Abraham's bosom than in Mary's; for it is in this last that our Lord has placed His throne,"—*Ne credideris majoris esse felicitatis habitare in sinu*

Abrahæ quam in sinu Mariæ, cum in eo Dominus posuerit thronum suum.

The reprobate, on the contrary, putting all their trust in themselves, only eat with the prodigal what the swine eat. They eat earth like the toads, and, like the children of the world, they love only visible and external things. They have no relish for the sweetnesses of Mary's bosom. They have not that feeling of a certain resting-place, and a sure confidence, which the predestinate feel in the holy Virgin, their good Mother. They are miserably attached to their outward hunger, as St. Gregory says, and make not so much as a pretence of having any taste for the sweetness which is prepared within themselves, and within Jesus and Mary.

5. Lastly, the predestinate keep the ways of our Blessed Lady, their good Mother; that is to say, they imitate her. It is in this point that they are truly happy and truly devout, and carry more especially the mark of their predestination. This good Mother says to them, *Beati qui custodiunt vias meas*; that is to say, "Blessed are they who practise my virtues, and with the help of divine grace walk in the footsteps of my life. During life they are happy in this world, through the abundance of graces and sweetnesses which I impart to them from my fulness, and more abundantly than to others, who do not imitate me so closely. They are happy in their death, which is mild and tranquil, and at which I am ordinarily present myself, that I myself may conduct them to the joys of eternity; and, lastly, they shall be happy in eternity; for never has any one of my good servants been lost, who imitated my virtues during life."

The reprobate, on the contrary, are unhappy during their life, at their death, and for eternity, because they do not imitate our Lady in her virtues, but content themselves with sometimes being enrolled in her confraternities, reciting some prayers in her honour, or going through some other exterior devotion. O holy Virgin, my good Mother, how happy are those (I repeat it with the transports of my heart),—how happy are those who, not letting themselves be seduced by a false devotion towards you, faithfully keep your ways, your counsels, and your orders! But how unhappy and accursed are those who abuse your devotion, and keep not the commandments of your Son: *Maledicti omnes qui declinant a mandatis tuis*!—"Cursed are all who fall from Thy commandments."

Oil painting of The Virgin of the Navigators, by Alejo Fernández (1535), Seville, Spain. Seamen and sailors would pray before this image prior to setting out to sea.

CHAPTER 9

Charitable Duties of Our Blessed Lady Towards her Faithful Servants

L et us now turn to look at the charitable duties which our Blessed
Lady, as the best of all Mothers, fulfils for the faithful servants who
have given themselves to her after the manner I have described, and
according to the figure of Jacob.

First Charitable Duty: Love of a True Mother

She loves them: *Ego diligentes me diligo*,—"I love those who love me." She
loves them (1) because she is their true Mother; and a mother loves her
child, the fruit of her entrails; (2) she loves them out of gratitude, because
they effectively love her as their good Mother; (3) she loves them because,
being predestinate, God loves them,—*Jacob dilexi, Esau autem odio habui*;
(4) she loves them because they are all consecrated to her, and are her possession and her inheritance,—*In Israel hæreditare*.

She loves them tenderly, and more tenderly than all other mothers put
together. Throw, if you can, all the natural love which all the mothers of
the world have for their children, into the one heart of one mother for one
only child. Surely that mother will love that child immensely. Nevertheless
it is true that Mary loves her children yet more tenderly than that mother
would love that child of hers.

Rebecca: The Figure of Mary

She does not love them only with affection, but with efficacy. Her love for them
is active and effective, equal to that of Rebecca for Jacob, and far beyond it.

See what this good Mother, of whom Rebecca was but the type, does to
obtain for her children the blessing of our Heavenly Father.

1. She is on the look-out, as Rebecca was, for favourable occasions to do
them good, to aggrandise and enrich them. She sees clearly in God all goods
and evils, all prosperous and adverse fortunes, the blessings and the cursings
of God; and then she so disposes things from afar, that she may exempt her
servants from all sorts of evils, and heap upon them all sorts of goods; so

that if there is a good fortune to make in God by the fidelity of a creature to any high employment, it is certain that Mary will procure that good fortune for some of her true children and servants, and will give them the grace to go through it with fidelity. It is a Saint who says, *Ipsa procurat negotia nostra.*

2. She also gives her clients good counsels, as Rebecca did to Jacob, *Fili mi, acquiesce consiliis meis,*—"My son, follow my counsels." Among other counsels, she inspires them to bring her the two kids; that is to say, their body and soul, in order to consecrate them, to make a pottage agreeable to God, and to do every thing which Jesus Christ her Son has taught by His words and His examples. If it is not by herself that she gives these counsels, it is by the ministry of the Angels, who have no greater honour or pleasure than to descend to earth to obey any of her commandments, and to succour any of her servants.

3. When they have brought to her and consecrated to her their body and soul, and all that depends on them, without excepting any thing, what does that good Mother do? Just what Rebecca did of old with the two kids Jacob brought her. (a) She kills them, and makes them die to the old Adam. (b) She flays, and strips them of their natural skin, their natural inclinations, self-love, their own will, and all attachment to creatures. (c) She cleanses them of their spots, their vilenesses, and their sins. (d) She dresses them to the taste of God, and to His greatest glory; and as it is Mary alone who knows perfectly what that divine taste is, and what that greatest glory of the Most High, it is Mary alone who, without making any mistake, can accommodate and dress our body and soul for that taste infinitely exalted, and for that glory infinitely hidden.

4. This good Mother, having received the perfect offering which we make to her of ourselves, our own merits and satisfactions, by the devotion I am describing, strips us of our old garments; she makes us her own, and so makes us worthy to appear before our heavenly Father.

- She clothes us in the clean, new, precious, and perfumed garments of Esau the elder,—that is, of Jesus Christ her Son,—whom she keeps in her house,—that is to say, whom she has in her own power. She is the treasurer and eternal dispenser of the merits and virtues of her Son, which she gives and communicates to whom she wills, when she wills, as she wills, and in such quantity as she wills; as we have seen before.

- She covers the neck and hands of her servants with the skins of the kids she killed; that is to say, she adorns them with the merits and value of her own proper actions. She kills and mortifies, it is true, all that is impure and imperfect in them, but she neither loses nor dissipates one atom of the good which grace has done there. On the contrary, she preserves and augments it, to make it the ornament and the strength of their neck and their hands; that is to say, to fortify them, and to help them to carry the yoke of the Lord, which is worn upon the neck, and to work great things for the glory of God, and the salvation of their poor brethren.

- She bestows a new perfume and a new grace upon their garments and adornments, in communicating to them her own garments, merits, and virtues, which she bequeathed to them by her testament, when she died; as said a holy religious of the last century, who died in the odour of sanctity, and learnt this by revelation. Thus all her domestics, faithful servants and slaves, are doubly clad in the garments of her Son and in her own,—*Omnes domestici vestiti sunt duplicibus*,—"All her domestics are clothed in double clothing." It is on this account that they have nothing to fear from the cold of Jesus Christ, who is white as snow,—a cold which the reprobate, all naked, and stripped of the merits of Jesus and Mary, cannot for one moment bear.

- Finally, she enables them to obtain the blessing of our Heavenly Father, though, being but the youngest born and indeed only adopted children, they have no natural right to have it. With these garments all new, most precious, and of most fragrant odour, and with their body and soul well prepared and dressed, they draw near with confidence to the Father's bed of repose. He understands and distinguishes their voice, which is the voice of the sinner; He touches their hands, covered with skins; He smells the good odour of their clothes; He eats with joy of that which Mary their Mother has dressed for Him, recognising in them the merits and the good odour of His Son and of His holy Mother. First, then, He gives them His double benediction, the benediction of the dew of Heaven, *De rore cœlesti*,—that is to say, of divine grace, which is the seed of glory; *Benedixit nos in omni benedictione spiritali in Christo Jesu*; and then the benediction of the fat of the earth, *De pinguedine terræ*,—that is to say, the good Father gives them their daily bread, and a sufficient abundance of the goods of this world. Secondly, He makes them masters of their other brethren, the reprobate. But this primacy is not always apparent in the world, which passes in an instant, and where the reprobate are often masters,—*Peccatores effabuntur et gloriabuntur; vidi impium superexaltatum et elevatum.* But it is nevertheless a true primacy; and it will appear manifestly in the other world for all eternity, where the just, as the Holy Ghost says, shall reign over the nations, and command them,—*Dominabuntur populis.* Thirdly, His Majesty, not content with blessing them in their persons and their goods, blesses also those who shall bless them, and curses those who shall curse and persecute them.

Second Charitable Duty: Provider in Spiritual and Temporal Necessities

The second duty which our Blessed Lady fulfils towards her faithful servants is, that she furnishes them with every thing, both for their body and their soul. She gives them double clothing, as we have just seen. She gives them to eat the most exquisite meats of the table of God; for she gives them to eat the bread of life, which she herself has formed. *A generationibus meis implemini,*—My dear children, she says, under the name of divine Wisdom, be filled with my generations; that is to say, with Jesus, the fruit of life, whom I have brought into the world for you. *Venite, comedite panem meum et bibite vinum quod miscui vobis; comedite, et bibite, et inebriamini, carissimi,*—Come, she repeats to them in another place, eat my bread, which is Jesus, and drink the wine of His love, which I have mixed for you. As it is Mary who is the treasurer and dispenser of the gifts and graces of the Most High, she gives a good portion, and indeed the best portion, to nourish and maintain her children and her servants. They are fattened on the Living Bread. They are inebriated on the wine which brings forth virgins. They are borne at the bosom of Mary,—*Ad ubera portabimini.* They have such facility in carrying the yoke of Jesus Christ, that they feel nothing of its weight, because of the oil of devotion which has made it soften and decay,—*Jugum eorum putrescere faciet a facie olei.*

Third Charitable Duty: Guide and Counsel

The third good which our Lady does to her servants is, that she conducts and directs them according to the will of her Son. Rebecca guided her little Jacob, and gave him good advice from time to time; either to draw upon himself the blessing of his father, or to avert from himself the hatred and persecution of his brother Esau. Mary, who is the Star of the Sea, leads all her faithful servants to a good port. She shows them the paths of eternal life. She makes them avoid the dangerous places. She conducts them by her hand along the paths of justice. She steadies them when they are about to fall; she lifts them up when they have fallen. She reproves them like a charitable mother when they fail; and sometimes she even lovingly chastises them. Can a child obedient to Mary, his foster-mother and his enlightened guide, go astray in the paths of eternity? *Ipsam sequens non devias,*—"If you follow her," says St. Bernard, "you cannot wander from the road." Fear not, therefore, that a true child of Mary can be deceived by the evil one, or fall into any formal heresy. There where the guidance of Mary is, neither the evil spirit with his illusions, nor the heretics with their subtleties, can ever come,—*Ipsâ tenente, non corruis.*

Fourth Charitable Duty: Protection and Defence

The fourth good office which our Lady renders to her children and faithful servants is, to protect and defend them. Rebecca, by her cares and artifices, delivered Jacob from all the dangers in which he found himself, and particularly from the death which his brother Esau would have inflicted on him, because of the envy and hatred which he bore him; as Cain did of old to his brother Abel. Mary, the good Mother of the predestinate, hides them under the wings of her protection, as a hen hides her chickens. She speaks, she humbles herself, she condescends to all their weaknesses, to secure them from the hawk and the vulture. She puts herself round about them, and she accompanies them, like an army in battle array, *ut castrorum acies ordinata.* Shall a man, who has an army of a hundred thousand soldiers around him, fear his enemies? A faithful servant of Mary, surrounded by her protection and her imperial power, has still less to fear. This good Mother and powerful princess of the heavens would rather despatch battalions of millions of angels to succour one of her servants than that it should ever be said that a faithful servant of Mary, who trusted in her, had had to succumb to the malice, the number, and the vehemence of his enemies.

Fifth Charitable Duty: Intercession and Mediation

Lastly, the fifth and the greatest good which the sweet Mary procures for her faithful clients is, to intercede for them with her Son, and to appease

Him by her prayers. She unites them to Him with a most intimate union, and she keeps them unshaken in that union.

Rebecca made Jacob come near to his father's bed. The good man touched him, embraced him, and even kissed him with joy, being content and satisfied with the well-dressed viands which he had brought him; and having smelt with much contentment the exquisite perfume of his garments, he cried out, *Ecce odor filii mei sicut odor agri pleni, cui benedixit Dominus,*—"Behold the odour of my son, which is like the odour of a full field that the Lord hath blest." This odour of the full field which charms the heart of the Father is nothing else than the odour of the virtues and merits of Mary, who is a field full of grace, where God the Father has sown His only Son, as a grain of the wheat of the elect. Oh, how a child, perfumed with the good odour of Mary, is welcome with Jesus Christ, who is the Father of the world to come! Oh, how promptly and how perfectly is such a child united to his Lord! But we have shown this at length already.

Furthermore, after Mary has heaped her favours upon her children and faithful servants, and has obtained for them the benediction of her Heavenly Father, and union with Jesus Christ, she preserves them in Jesus, and Jesus in them: She takes care of them, watches over them always, for fear they should lose the grace of God, and fall back into the snares of their enemies. *In plenitudine detinet,*—she detains the Saints in their fulness, and makes them persevere to the end, as we have seen.

This is the interpretation of [the history of Jacob and Esau] that great and ancient figure of predestination and reprobation, so unknown, and so full of mysteries.

CHAPTER 10

Admirable Effects of the Perfect Consecration to Jesus by Mary

My dear brother, be sure that, if you are faithful to the interior and exterior practices of this devotion, which I will point out, the following effects will take place in your soul:

1. By the light which the Holy Ghost will give you by His dear Spouse, Mary, you will understand your own evil, your corruption, and your incapacity for any thing good, which is not God's free gift to us, either as Author of nature or of grace. In consequence of this knowledge, you will despise yourself. You will only think of yourself with horror. You will regard yourself as a snail, that spoils every thing with its slime; or a toad, that poisons every thing with its venom; or as a spiteful serpent, only seeking to deceive. In other words, the humble Mary will communicate to you a portion of her profound humility, which will make you despise yourself, despise nobody else, but love to be despised yourself.

2. Our Blessed Lady will give you also a portion of her faith, which was the greatest of all faiths that ever were on earth, greater than the faith of all the Patriarchs, Prophets, Apostles, and Saints put together. Now that she is reigning in the heavens, she has no longer this faith, because she sees all things clearly in God by the light of glory. Nevertheless, with the consent of the Most High, in entering into glory she has not lost her faith. She has kept it, in order that she may keep it in the Church Militant for her faithful servants. The more, then, you gain the favour of that august Princess and faithful Virgin, the more will you go by pure faith in all your conduct; a pure faith which will make you hardly care at all about the sensible and the extraordinary; a lively faith animated by charity, which will enable you to perform all your actions from the motive of pure love; a faith firm and immovable as a rock, through which you will rest quiet and constant in the midst of storms and hurricanes; a faith active and piercing, which, like a mysterious pass-key, will give you entrance into all the mysteries of Jesus, into the Last Ends of man, and into the Heart of God Himself; a courageous faith, which will enable you to undertake and carry out without hesitation great things for God and for the salvation of souls; lastly, a faith which will be your blazing torch, your divine life, your hidden treasure of divine wisdom, and your omnipotent arm, which you will use to enlighten those who are in the darkness of the shadow of death, to inflame those who are lukewarm and who have need of the heated gold of charity, to give life to those who are dead in sin, to teach and overthrow, by your meek and powerful words, the hearts of marble and the cedars of Lebanon, and finally, to resist the devil and all the enemies of salvation.

3. This Mother of fair love will take away from your heart all scruple and all disorder of servile fear. She will open and enlarge it to run the way of her Son's commandments with the holy liberty of the children of God. She will introduce into it pure love, of which she has the treasure; so that you shall no longer be guided by fear, as hitherto, in your dealings with the God of charity, but by pure love. You will look on Him as your good Father, whom you will be incessantly trying to please, and with whom you will converse confidently, as a child with its tender father. If unfortunately you offend Him, you will at once humble yourself before Him. You will ask His pardon with great lowliness, but at the same time you will stretch your hand out to Him with simplicity; and you will raise yourself up lovingly, without trouble or disquietude, and go on your way to Him without discouragement.

4. Our Blessed Lady will fill you with a great confidence in God and in herself: (a) because you will not be approaching to Jesus by yourself, but always by that good Mother; (b) because, as you have given her all your merits, graces, and satisfactions, to dispose of at her will, she will communicate to you her virtues, and will clothe you in her merits, so that you will be able to say to God with confidence, "Behold Mary Thy handmaid; be it done unto me according to Thy word,"—*Ecce ancilla Domini, fiat mihi secundum verbum tuum*; (c) because, as you have given yourself entirely to her, body and soul, she, who is liberal with the liberal, and more liberal even than the liberal, will in return give herself to you in a marvellous but real manner, so that you may say to her with assurance, *Tuus sum ego, salvum me fac*,—"I am thine, holy Virgin; save me:" or, as I have said before, with the Beloved Disciple, *Accepi te in mea*,—"I have taken thee, holy Mother, for all my goods." You may also say with St. Bonaventure, *Ecce, Domina, salvatrix mea, fiducialiter agam et non timebo, quia fortitudo mea, et laus mea in Domino es tu*; and in another place, *Tuus totus ego sum, et* *omnia mea tua sunt; O virgo gloriosa, super omnia benedicta, ponam te ut signaculum super cor meum, quia fortis est ut mors dilectio tua.* "My dear Mistress, who saves me, I will have confidence and will not fear, because you are my strength and my praise in the Lord. ... I am altogether yours, and all that I have belongs to you; O glorious Virgin, blessed above all created things! I will put you as a seal upon my heart, because your love is as strong as death."

You may say to God, in the sentiments of the prophet, *Domine, non est exaltatum cor meum, neque elati sunt oculi mei; neque ambulavi in magnis, neque in mirabilibus super me, si non humiliter sentiebam; sed exaltavi animam meam: sicut ablactatus est super matre tua, ita retributio in anima mea,*—"Lord, my heart and my eyes have no right to extol themselves, or to be proud, or to seek great and wonderful things. Yet even in this I am not humble; but I have lifted up and encouraged my soul by confidence: I am like a child, weaned from the pleasures of earth, and resting on its mother's lap; and it is on that lap that all good things come to me" (see Psalm 130). (d) What will still further increase your confidence in her is, that you will have less confidence in yourself. You have given her, in trust, all you have of good about you, that she may have it and keep it; and so all the trust you once had in yourself has become an increase of confidence in her, who is your treasure. Oh, what confidence and what consolation is this for a soul, who can say that the treasure of God, where He has been pleased to put all He had most precious, is his own treasure also! *Ipsa est thesaurus Domini.* It was a Saint who said she was the treasure of the Lord.

5. The soul of our Blessed Lady will communicate itself to you, to glorify the Lord. Her spirit will enter into the place of yours, to rejoice in God her salvation, provided only that you are faithful to the practices of this devotion. *Sit in singulis anima Mariæ, ut magnificet Dominum: sit in singulis spiritus Mariæ, ut exultet in Deo* (St. Ambrose),—"Let the soul of Mary be in each of us to glorify the Lord: let the spirit of Mary be in each of us to rejoice in God." Ah! when will the happy time come, said a holy man of our own days, who was all absorbed in Mary,—ah! when will the happy time come, when the divine Mary will be established mistress and queen of hearts, in order that she may subject them fully to the empire of her great and holy Jesus? When will souls breathe Mary, as the body breathes air? When that time comes, wonderful things will happen in those lowly places, where the Holy Ghost, finding His dear Spouse as it were reproduced in souls, shall come in with abundance, and fill them full to overflowing with His gifts, and particularly with the gift of wisdom, to work the miracles of grace. My dear brother, when will that happy time, that age of Mary, come, when souls, losing themselves in the abyss of her interior, shall become living copies of Mary, to love and glorify Jesus? That time will not come until men shall know and practise this devotion which I am teaching. *Ut adveniat regnum tuum, adveniat regnum Mariæ.*

6. If Mary, who is the tree of life, is well cultivated in our soul by fidelity to the practices of this devotion, she will bear her fruit in her own time, and her fruit is none other than Jesus Christ. How many devout souls do I see who seek Jesus Christ, some by one way or by one practice, and others by other ways and other practices; and after they have toiled much throughout the night, they say, *Per totam noctem laborantes nihil cepimus,*—"We have toiled all night, and have taken nothing"! We may say to them, *Laborastis multum, et intulistis parum,*—"You have laboured much, and gained little:" Jesus Christ is yet feeble in you. But by that immaculate way of Mary, and that divine practice which I am teaching, we toil during the day; we toil in a holy place; we toil but little. There is no night in Mary, because there is no sin, nor even the slightest shade. Mary is a holy place, and the holy of holies where Saints are formed and moulded. Take notice, if you please, that I say the Saints are moulded in Mary. There is a great difference between making a figure in relief by blows of hammer and chisel, and making a figure by throwing it into a mould. Statuaries and sculptors labour much to make figures in the first manner; but to make them in the second manner, they work little, and do their work quickly.

> *If Mary, who is the tree of life, is well cultivated in our soul by fidelity to the practices of this devotion, she will bear her fruit in her own time, and her fruit is none other than Jesus Christ.*

St. Augustine calls our Blessed Lady *forma Dei,*—"the mould of God:" *Si formam Dei te appellem, digna existis,*—"The mould fit to cast and mould gods." He who is cast in this mould is presently formed and moulded in Jesus Christ, and Jesus Christ in him. At a slight expense and in a short time he will become God, because he has been cast in the same mould which has formed a God.

It seems to me that I can very aptly compare directors and devout persons, who wish to form Jesus Christ in themselves or others by different practices from this, to sculptors who trust in their own professional skill, ingenuity, or art, and so give an infinity of hammerings and chisellings to a hard stone or a piece of badly polished wood, to make an image of Jesus Christ out of it. Sometimes they do not succeed in giving any thing like the natural expression of Jesus, either from having no knowledge or experience of the Person of Jesus, or from some blow awkwardly given, which has spoiled the work. But for those who embrace the secret of grace which I am revealing to them, I may reasonably compare them to founders and casters, who have discovered the beautiful mould of Mary, where Jesus was naturally and divinely formed; and without trusting to their own skill, but only in the goodness of the mould, they cast themselves and lose themselves in Mary, to become the portraits of Jesus Christ after nature.

Oh, beautiful and true comparison! but who will comprehend it? I desire that you may, my dear brother. But remember that we only cast in a mould what is melted and liquid; that is to say, you must destroy and melt down in yourself the old Adam to become the new one in Mary.

7. By this practice, faithfully observed, you will give Jesus more glory in a month than by any other practice, however difficult, in many years; and I give the following reasons for it.

First, because, doing your actions by our Blessed Lady, as this practice teaches you, you abandon your own intentions and operations, although good and known, to lose yourself, so to speak, in the intentions of the Blessed Virgin, although they are unknown. Thus you enter by participation into the sublimity of her intentions, which are so pure, that she gives more glory to God by the least of her actions—for example, in twirling her distaff or pointing her needle—than St. Lawrence by his cruel martyrdom on his gridiron, or even all the Saints by all their heroic actions put together. It was thus that, during her sojourn here below, she acquired such an unspeakable aggregate of graces and merits, that it were easier to count the stars of the firmament, the drops of water in the sea, or the grains of sand upon its shore, than her merits and graces. Thus it was that she gave more glory to God than all the Angels and Saints have given Him, or ever will give Him. O prodigy of a Mary! thou canst not help but do prodigies of grace in souls that wish to lose themselves altogether in thee!

Second, because the soul in this practice counts as nothing whatever it thinks or does of itself; and only puts its trust, and takes its pleasure, in the dispositions of Mary, when it approaches Jesus, or even speaks to Him. Thus it practises humility far more than the souls who act of themselves, and lean, with however imperceptible a complacency, on their own dispositions. But if the soul acts more humbly, it therefore glorifies God more highly; and He is only perfectly glorified by the humble, and those that are little and lowly in heart.

Third, because our Blessed Lady, wishing by her great charity to receive the present of our actions in her virginal hands, gives them an admirable beauty and splendour. Moreover, she offers them herself to Jesus Christ, and without difficulty; and our Lord is thus more glorified by them than if we offered them by our own criminal hands.

Lastly, because you never think of Mary without Mary, in your place, thinking of God. You never praise or honour Mary without Mary praising and honouring God. Mary is altogether relative to God; and, indeed, I might well call her the relation to God. She only exists with reference to God. She is the echo of God, who says nothing, repeats nothing, but God. If you say 'Mary,' she says 'God.' St. Elizabeth praised Mary, and called her blessed, because she had believed. Mary, the faithful echo of God, at once intoned *Magnificat anima mea Dominum*,—"My soul doth magnify the Lord." That which Mary did then, she does daily now. When we praise her, love her, honour her, or give any thing to her, it is God who is praised, God who is loved, God who is glorified. We give then to God by Mary and in Mary.

CHAPTER 11

Particular Practices of this Devotion

External Practices

Although what is essential in this devotion consists in the interior, we must not fail to unite to the inward practice certain external observances. *Hæc oportet facere, et illa non omittere.* We must do the one, yet not leave the other undone, both because the outward practices well performed aid the inward ones, and because they make a man remember, by reminding his senses, what he has done or ought to do; and also because they are suitable to edify our neighbour, who sees them, which inward practices cannot do. Let no worldling then or critic sneer at this. Let them not say that because true devotion is in the heart, we must avoid external devotion; or that devotion ought to be hidden, and that there may be vanity in showing it. I answer with my Master, that men should see our good works, that they may glorify our Father, who is in Heaven; not, as St. Gregory says, that we ought to perform our actions and exterior devotions to please men and to get praise,—that would be vanity,—but that we should sometimes do them before men, with the view of pleasing God, and glorifying Him thereby, without caring either for the contempt or the praise of men.

I will only allude briefly to some exterior practices, which I do not call 'exterior' because we do them without any interior, but because they have something outward about them, to distinguish them from those which are purely inward.

• First Practice

Those who wish to enter into this particular devotion, which is not at present erected into a confraternity, though that were to be wished,—after having, as I said in the first part of this preparation for the reign of Jesus Christ, employed twelve days, at least, in emptying themselves of the spirit of the world, which is contrary to the spirit of Jesus Christ,—should employ three weeks in filling themselves with Jesus Christ by the holy Virgin. They should pursue the following order:

During the first week they should employ all their prayers and pious actions in asking for a knowledge of themselves, and for contrition of their sins; and they should do this in a spirit of humility. For that end they can, if they choose, meditate on what I have said before of our inward corruption. They can look upon themselves during the six days of this week as snails, crawling things, toads, swine, serpents, and unclean animals; or they can reflect on those three considerations of St. Bernard, the vileness of our origin, the dishonours of our present state, and our ending as the food of worms. They should pray our Lord and the Holy Ghost to enlighten them; and for that end they might use the ejaculations, *Domine, ut videam*, or *Noverim me*, or *Veni Sancte Spiritus*; and they may say daily the *Ave maris stella*, and the litany of the Holy Ghost.

During the second week they should apply themselves, during all their prayers and works each day, to know the Blessed Virgin. They should ask this knowledge of the Holy Ghost; they should read and meditate what we have said about it. They should recite, as in the first week, the litany of the Holy Ghost and the *Ave maris stella*, and in addition a Rosary daily, or, if not a whole Rosary, at least a chaplet, for the intention of impetrating more knowledge of Mary.

During the third week, they should apply themselves to know Jesus Christ. They can meditate upon what we have said about Him, and say the prayer of St. Augustine, which they will find in the first part of this treatise. They can, with the same Saint, repeat a hundred times a day, *Noverim te*,—"Lord, that I might know Thee!" or *Domine, ut videam*,—"Lord, that I might see who Thou art!" They shall recite, as in the preceding weeks, the litany of the Holy Ghost and the *Ave maris stella*, and they shall add daily the litany of the Holy Name of Jesus. At the end of the three weeks they shall confess and communicate, with the intention of giving themselves to Jesus Christ, in the quality of slaves of love, by the hands of Mary. After communion, which they should try to make according to the method given farther on, they should recite the formula of their consecration, which they will find afterwards. They ought to write it, or have it written, unless it is printed; and they should sign it the same day they have made it. It would be well also that on that day they should pay some tribute to Jesus Christ and our Blessed Lady, either as a penance for their past unfaithfulness to the vows of their Baptism, or in testimony of their dependence and allegiance to the domain of Jesus and Mary. This tribute ought to be according to the devotion and capacity of every one, as a fast, a mortification, an alms, or a candle. If they had but a pin to give in homage, yet gave it with a good heart, it would be enough for Jesus, who looks only at the good-will. Once a year at least, on the same day, they should renew the same consecration, observing the same practices during the three weeks. They might also once a month, or even once a day, renew what they have done by these few words: *Tuus totus ego sum, et omnia mea tua sunt*,— "I am all for Thee, and all I have belongs to Thee, O my sweet Jesus, by Mary Thy holy Mother."

• Second Practice

They may recite every day of their life, without however making any burden of it, the Little Corona of the Blessed Virgin, composed of three Our Fathers and twelve Hail Marys, in honour of our Lady's twelve privileges and grandeurs. This is a very ancient practice, for it has its foundation in the holy Scriptures. St. John saw a woman crowned with twelve stars, clothed with the sun, and holding the moon under her feet; and this woman, according to the interpreters, was the most holy Virgin. There are many ways of saying this Corona well; but it would be too long to enter upon them. The Holy Ghost will teach them to those who are the most faithful to this devotion. Nevertheless, to say it quite simply we should begin by saying, *Dignare me laudare te, Virgo sacrata, da mihi virtutem contra hostes tuos*. After that we should say the Credo, and then a Pater with four Aves, and then one Gloria Patri; then another Pater, four Aves, and one Gloria Patri, and so on with the rest; and at the end we should say the *Sub tuum præsidium*.

> ### SUB TUUM PRÆSIDIUM
> We fly to thy patronage, O holy Mother of God; despise not our petitions in our necessities, but deliver us always from all dangers, O glorious and blessed Virgin. ***Amen.***

• Third Practice

It is a most glorious and praiseworthy thing, and very useful to those who have thus made themselves slaves of Jesus and Mary, that they should wear, as a badge of their loving slavery, little iron chains, blessed with the proper benediction.[1]

It is perfectly true that these external badges are not essential, and a person who has embraced this devotion may very well go without them; nevertheless, I cannot refrain from warmly praising those who, after having shaken off the shameful chains of the slavery of the devil, in which original sin, and perhaps actual sins, had engaged them, have voluntarily surrendered themselves to the glorious slavery of Jesus Christ, and glory with St. Paul in being in chains for Jesus; chains a thousand times more glorious and precious, though of iron, than all the golden collars of emperors.

> *Once there was nothing more infamous on earth than the Cross, and now that wood is the most glorious boast of Christianity.*

Once there was nothing more infamous on earth than the Cross, and now that wood is the most glorious boast of Christianity. Let us say the same of the irons of slavery. There was nothing more ignominious among the ancients; nothing more shameful even now among the heathen. But among Christians there is nothing more illustrious than the chains of Jesus; for they unchain us, and preserve us from the infamous fetters of sin and the devil. They set us at liberty, and chain us to Jesus and Mary; not by compulsion and constraint, like galley-slaves, but by charity and love, like children. *Traham eos in vinculis charitatis,*—"I will draw them to Me," said God by the mouth of the prophet, "by the chains of love." These chains are as strong as death, and they are in a certain sense strongest in those who are faithful in carrying these glorious badges to their death. For, though death destroys their bodies in bringing

---

1. *Note from the French.* It may be thought that, since the time of the venerable servant of God, certain decrees of the Congregation of the Index have absolutely condemned this usage; but whatever may be the precise extent of the prohibition intended by these decrees, there seems to be nothing in them formally interdicting the using of little chains to *private persons.* We may see at the end of Collet's Life of Boudon the remarks of that theologian, justifying the pious Archdeacon of Evreux from the criticisms of which he was the object, by the occasion of his treatise *Le saint Esclavage de la Sainte Vierge.* He cites the decrees which he read in the edition of the Index of 1758, and which have been repeated in the subsequent editions. The words of the Index are as follows: "Prohibentur imagines, numismata insculpta pro confraternitatibus mancipiorum Matris Dei, italice schiavi della Madre di Dio, sodales catenatos exprimentia. Item libelli in quibus eisdem confraternitatibus regulæ præscribentur. Confraternitates autem quæ catenulas distribuunt confratribus et consororibus, brachiis et collo circumponendas atque gestandas, ut eo signo beatissimæ Virgini mancipatos se esse profiteantur, et quarum institutum in eo mancipatu præcipuè versatur, damnantur et exstinguuntur. Societatibus verò quæ ritum aliquem aut quodcumque aliud ad mancipatum ejusmodi pertinens adhibent, præcipitur ut id statim rejiciant" (Index, Decreta generalia, § 3, no. 3).

them to corruption, it does not destroy the chains of their slavery, which, being of iron, do not corrupt so easily. Perhaps, at the day of the resurrection of the body, the grand last judgment, these chains shall still be round their bones, and shall make a part of their glory, and be transmuted into chains of light and splendour. Happy, then, a thousand times happy, the illustrious slaves of Jesus, who wear their chains even to the tomb!

The following are the reasons for wearing these little chains:

First, it is to remind the Christian of the vows and engagements of his Baptism, of the perfect renewal he has made of them by this devotion, and of the strict obligation under which he is to be faithful to them. As the man who shapes his course more often by the senses than by pure faith easily forgets his obligations towards God, unless he has some outward thing to remind him of them, these little chains serve marvellously to remind the Christian of the chains of sin, and of the slavery of the devil, from which Baptism has delivered him, and of the dependence on Jesus which he has vowed to Him in Baptism, and of the ratification of it which he has made by the renewal of his vows. One of the reasons why so few Christians think of their baptismal vows, and live with as much license as if they had promised no more to God than the heathen, is because they do not wear any external badge to make them remember it.

Secondly, it is to show that we are not ashamed of the servitude and slavery of Jesus Christ, and that we renounce the slavery of the world, sin, and the devil.

Thirdly, it is to guarantee ourselves from the chains of sin and the devil, and to be beforehand with them; for we must wear either the chains of iniquity, or the chains of charity and salvation: *Vincula peccatorum aut vincula charitatis.* O my dear brother, let us break the chains of sin and of sinners, of the world and of worldliness, of the devil and his ministers; and let us cast far from us their depressing yoke: *Dirumpamus vincula eorum, et projiciamus a nobis jugum ipsorum.* Let us put our feet, to use the terms of the Holy Ghost, into His glorious irons, and our neck into His collars: *Injice pedem tuum in compedes illius, et in torques illius collum tuum; subjice humerum tuum et porta illam, et ne acedieris vinculis ejus.* You will remark that the Holy Ghost, before saying these words, prepares a soul for them, lest it should reject His important counsel. See His words: *Audi, fili, et accipe consilium intellectus, et ne abjicias consilia mea,*—"Hearken, My son, and receive a counsel of understanding, and reject not My counsel."

You would wish, my very dear friend, that I should here unite myself to the Holy Ghost to give you the same counsel with Him. *Vincula illius alligatura salutis,*—His chains are chains of salvation. As Jesus Christ on the cross ought to draw all things to Him, with their will or against it, He will draw the reprobate by the chains of their sins, that He may chain them like galley-slaves and devils to His eternal anger and revengeful justice. But He will, and particularly in these latter times, draw the predestinate by the chains of charity. *Omnia traham ad meipsum. Traham eos in vinculis charitatis.* These loving slaves of Jesus Christ, "the chained of Christ,"—*Vincti Christi,*—can wear their chains either on their neck or on their feet. Father Vincent Caraffa, seventh general of the Jesuits, who died in the odour of sanctity, in the year 1643, used to wear a circle of iron round his feet as a mark of his servitude; and said that his only pain was that he could not publicly drag a chain.

The Mother Agnes of Jesus, of whom we have spoken before, used to wear an iron chain round her body. Others have worn it round their neck, in penance for the collars of pearls which they have worn in the world; while others have worn it round their arms, to remind themselves, in their manual labours, that they were slaves of Jesus Christ.

• Fourth Practice

Those who undertake this holy slavery should have a very special devotion to the great mystery of the Incarnation of the Word on the 25th of March. Indeed, the Incarnation is the proper mystery of this practice, inasmuch as it was a devotion inspired by the Holy Ghost, first, to honour and imitate the ineffable dependence which God the Son has been pleased to have on Mary, for His Father's glory and our salvation; which dependence particularly appears in this mystery, where Jesus is a captive and a slave in the bosom of the divine Mary, and depends upon her for all things; secondly, to thank God for the incomparable graces He has given Mary, and particularly for having chosen her to be His most holy Mother, which choice was made in this mystery. These are the two principal ends of the slavery of Jesus in Mary.

Have the goodness to observe that I generally say 'the slave of Jesus in Mary,' 'the slavery of Mary in Jesus.' I might, in good truth, as many have done before, say 'the slave of Mary,' 'the slavery of the holy Virgin;' but I think it is better to say 'the slave of Jesus in Mary,' as Mr. Tronson, superior general of the seminary in St. Sulpice, renowned for his rare prudence and consummate piety, counselled to an ecclesiastic who consulted him on the subject. The following were the reasons:

First, as we are living in an age of intellectual pride, and there are all round us numbers of puffed-up scholars and conceited and critical spirits, who have plenty to say against the best established and most solid practices of piety, it is better for us not to give them any needless occasion of criticism. Hence it is better for us to say 'the slavery of Jesus in Mary,' and to call ourselves the slaves of Jesus Christ rather than the slaves of Mary, taking the denomination of our devotion rather from its last end, which is Jesus Christ, than from the road and the means to the end, which Mary is; though I repeat that in truth we may do either, as I have done myself. For example: a man who goes from Orleans to Tours by way of Amboise may very well say that he is going to Amboise, or that he is going to Tours; that he is a traveller to Amboise, and a traveller to Tours; with this difference however, that Amboise is but his straight road to Tours, and that Tours only is the last end and term of his voyage.

A second reason is because the principal mystery we celebrate in honour of this devotion is the mystery of the Incarnation, where we can only see Jesus in Mary, and incarnate in her bosom. Hence it is more to the purpose to speak of the slavery of Jesus in Mary, and of Jesus residing and reigning in Mary, according to that beautiful prayer of so many great men, "O Jesus, living in Mary, come and live in us, in Thy spirit of sanctity," etc.

Another reason is because this manner of speaking sets forth still more the intimate union which there is between Jesus and Mary. They are so intimately united, that the one is altogether in the other. Jesus is altogether in Mary, and Mary is altogether in Jesus; or rather, she exists no more, but Jesus is all alone in her, and it were easier to separate the light from the sun than Mary from Jesus. So that we might call our Lord *Jesus of Mary*, and our Blessed Lady *Mary of Jesus*.

The time would not permit me to stop now to explain the excellences and grandeurs of the mysteries of Jesus living and reigning in Mary, in other words, of the Incarnation of the Word, I will content myself with saying these three words: We have here the first mystery of Jesus Christ,—the most hidden, the most exalted, and the least known. It is in this mystery that Jesus, in His Mother's womb, which is for that very reason called by the Saints the cabinet of the secrets of God, has, in concert with Mary, chosen all the elect.

It is in this mystery that He has wrought all the other mysteries of His life by the acceptance which He made of them. *Jesus ingrediens mundum dicit, Ecce venio, ut faciam voluntatem tuam.* Consequently this mystery is an abridgment of all mysteries, and contains the will and grace of all. Finally, this mystery is the throne of the mercy, of the liberality, and of the glory of God. It is the throne of His mercy for us, because, as we cannot approach Jesus but by Mary, we can only see Jesus and speak to Him by her intercession. Jesus, who always hears His dear Mother, always grants His grace and mercy to poor sinners. *Adeamus ergo cum fiduciâ ad thronum gratiæ.* It is the throne of His liberality for Mary, because, while the new Adam dwelt in that true terrestrial Paradise, He worked so many miracles in secret, that neither Angels nor men can comprehend them. It is on this account that the Saints call Mary the magnificence of God,—*Magnificentia Dei,*—as if God were only magnificent in Mary: *solummodò ibi magnificus Dominus.* It is the throne of His glory for His Father, because it is in Mary that Jesus Christ has calmed His Father, irritated against men, and that He has made restitution of the glory which sin ravished from Him, and that, by the sacrifice He made of His own will and of Himself, He has given Him more glory than ever the sacrifices of the Ancient Law could do, and He gives Him now an infinite glory, which He never could have received from man.

• Fifth Practice

Those who adopt this slavery ought also to have a great devotion to saying the Hail Mary (the Angelical Salutation). Few Christians, however enlightened, know the real price, merit, excellence, and necessity of the Hail Mary. It was necessary for the Blessed Virgin to appear several times to great and enlightened Saints, to show them the merit of it. She did so to St. Dominic, St. John Capistran, and the Blessed Alan de la Roche. They have composed entire works on the wonders and efficacy of that prayer for converting souls. They have loudly published and openly preached that, salvation having begun with the Hail Mary, the salvation of each one of us in particular is attached to that prayer. They tell us that it is that prayer which made the dry and barren earth bring forth the fruit of life; and that it is that prayer well said which makes the Word of God germinate in our souls, and bring forth Jesus Christ, the Fruit of life. They tell us that the Hail Mary is a heavenly dew for watering the earth, which is the soul, to make it bring forth its fruit in season; and that a soul which is not watered by that prayer bears no fruit, and brings forth only thorns and brambles, and is ready to be cursed.

Listen to what our Lady revealed to the Blessed Alan de la Roche, as he has recorded it in his book on the dignity of the Rosary: "Know, my son, and make all others know, that it is a probable and proximate sign of eternal damnation to have an aversion, a Iukewarmness, or a negligence, in saying the Angelical Salutation, which has repaired the whole world." *Scias enim et securè intelligas et inde latè omnibus notum facias, quod videlicet signum probabile est et propinquum æternæ damnationis horrere et acediari, ac negligere Salutationem Angelicam, totius mundi reparationem.* These are words at once terrible and consoling, and which we should find it hard to believe, if we had not that holy man for a guarantee, and St. Dominic before him, and many great men since. But we have also the experience of several ages; for it has always been remarked that those who wear the outward look of reprobation, like impious heretics and proud worldlings, hate or despise the Hail Mary or the Rosary.

Heretics still learn and say the Our Father, but not the Hail Mary, nor the Rosary. That is their horror. They would rather wear a serpent than a rosary.

> *The Hail Mary... is the most perfect compliment which you can make to Mary, because it is the compliment which the Most High sent her by an archangel, in order to gain her heart.*

The proud also, although Catholics, have the same inclinations as their father, Lucifer; and so have only contempt or indifference for the Hail Mary, and look at the Rosary as at a devotion which is only good for the ignorant and for those who cannot read. On the contrary it is an equally universal experience, that those who have otherwise great marks of predestination about them love and relish the Hail Mary, and delight in saying it. We always see the more a man is for God, the more he likes that prayer. This is what our Lady said also to the Blessed Alan, after the words which I have recently quoted. I do not know how it is, nor why, but nevertheless I well know that it is true; nor have I any better secret of knowing whether a person is for God than to examine if he likes to say the Hail Mary and the Rosary. I say, *if he likes*; for it may happen that a person may be under some natural inability to say it, or even a supernatural one; yet nevertheless he likes it always, and always inspires the same liking into others. O predestinate souls! slaves of Jesus in Mary! learn that the Hail Mary is the most beautiful of all prayers after the Our Father. It is the most perfect compliment which you can make to Mary, because it is the compliment which the Most High sent her by an archangel, in order to gain her heart; and it was so powerful over her heart by the secret charms of which it is so full, that in spite of her profound humility, she gave her consent to the Incarnation of the Word. It is by this compliment also that you will infallibly gain her heart, if you say it as you ought.

The Hail Mary well said, that is, with attention, devotion, and modesty, is, according to the Saints, the enemy of the devil, which puts him to flight, and the hammer which crushes him. It is the sanctification of the soul, the joy of Angels, the melody of the predestinate, the canticle of the New Testament, the pleasure of Mary, and the glory of the Most Holy Trinity. The Hail Mary is a heavenly dew which fertilises the soul. It is the chaste and loving kiss which we give to Mary. It is a vermilion rose which we present to her; a precious pearl we offer her; a chalice of divine ambrosial nectar which we hold to her. All these are comparisons of the Saints.

I pray you urgently, by the love I bear you in Jesus and Mary, not to content yourselves with saying the Little Corona of the Blessed Virgin, but a whole Chaplet; or even, if you have time, the whole Rosary every day. At the moment of your death, you will bless the day and hour in which you have followed my advice. Having thus sown in the benedictions of Jesus and Mary, you will reap eternal benedictions in heaven: *qui seminat in benedictionibus, de benedictionibus et metet.*

• Sixth Practice

To thank God for the graces He has given to our Lady, those who adopt this devotion will often say the Magnificat, as the Blessed Mary d'Oignies did, and many other Saints. It is the only prayer, the only work, which the holy Virgin composed, or rather which Jesus composed in her; for He spoke by her mouth. It is the greatest sacrifice of praise which God ever received from a pure creature in the law of grace. It is, on the one hand, the most humble and grateful, and on the other hand, the most sublime and exalted, of all canticles. There are in that song mysteries so great and hidden, that the Angels do not know them. The pious and erudite Gerson employed a great part of his life in composing works upon most difficult subjects; and yet it was only at the close of his career, and even then with trembling, that he undertook to comment on the Magnificat, so as to crown all his other works. He wrote a folio volume on it, and brings forward many admirable things about that beautiful and divine canticle. Among other things, he says that our Lady often repeated it herself, and especially for thanksgiving after Communion. The learned Benzonius, in explaining the same Magnificat, relates many miracles wrought by the virtue of it, and says that the devils tremble and fly when they hear these words: *Fecit potentiam in brachio suo, dispersit superbos mente cordis sui.*

• Seventh Practice

Those faithful servants of Mary, who adopt this devotion, ought always greatly to despise, to hate, and to eschew the corrupted world, and to make use of those practices of the contempt of the world which we have given in the first part of this treatise.

Interior Practices

Besides the external practices of the devotion which we have been describing so far, and which we must not omit through negligence or contempt, so far as the state and condition of each one will allow him to observe them, there are some very sanctifying interior practices for those whom the Holy Ghost calls to high perfection.

These may be expressed in four words: to do all our actions *by* Mary, *with* Mary, *in* Mary, and *for* Mary; so that we may do them all the more perfectly *by* Jesus, *with* Jesus, *in* Jesus, and *for* Jesus.

• All our Actions *by* Mary

We must do our actions *by* Mary; that is to say, we must obey her in all things, and in all things conduct ourselves by her spirit, which is the Holy Spirit of God. Those who are led by the Spirit of God are the children of God,—*Qui spiritu Dei aguntur, ii sunt filii Dei.* Those who are led by the spirit of Mary are the children of Mary, and consequently the children of God, as we have shown; and among so many clients of the Blessed Virgin, none are true or faithful but those who are led by her spirit. I have said that the spirit of Mary was the Spirit of God, because she was never led by her own spirit, but always by the Holy Ghost, who has rendered Himself so completely master of her, that He has become her own proper spirit. It is on this account that St. Ambrose says: *Sit in singulis Mariæ anima, ut magnificet Dominum; sit in singulis spiritus Mariæ, ut exsultet in Deo,*—"Let the soul of Mary be in each of us to magnify the Lord, and the spirit of Mary be in each of us to rejoice in God." A soul is happy indeed, when, like the good Jesuit lay brother, Alphonso Rodriguez, who died in the odour of sanctity, it is all possessed and over-ruled by the spirit of Mary, a spirit meek and strong, zealous and prudent, humble and courageous, pure and profound. In order that the soul may let itself be led by Mary's spirit, it must first of all renounce its own spirit, and its own proper lights and wills, before it does any thing. For example: it should do so before its prayer, before its saying or hearing Mass, and before communicating; because the darkness of our own spirit, and the malice of our own will and operation, if we follow them, however good they may appear to us, will put an obstacle to the spirit of Mary. Secondly, we must deliver ourselves to the spirit of Mary to be moved and influenced by it in the manner she chooses. We must put ourselves and leave ourselves in her virginal hands, like a tool in the grasp of a workman, like a lute in the hands of a skilful player. We must lose ourselves, and abandon ourselves to her, like a stone one throws into the sea. This must be done simply and in an instant, by one glance of the mind, by one little movement of the will, or even verbally, in saying, for example, I renounce myself; I give myself to thee, my dear Mother. We may not, perhaps, feel any sensible sweetness in this act of union, but it is not on that account the less real. It is just as if we were to say with equal sincerity, though without any sensible change in ourselves, what, may it please God, we never shall say, I give myself to the devil; we should not the less truly belong to the devil because we did not *feel* we belonged to him. Thirdly, we must, from time to time, both during and after the action, renew the same act and offering of union. The more we shall do so, the more we shall be sanctified; and we shall all the sooner attain to union with Jesus Christ, which always follows necessarily on our union with Mary, because the spirit of Mary is the spirit of Jesus.

• All our Actions *with* Mary

We must do our actions *with* Mary; that is to say, we must in all our actions regard Mary as an accomplished model of every virtue and perfection which the Holy Ghost has formed in a pure creature, for us to imitate according to our little measure. We must therefore in every action consider how Mary has done it, or how she would have done it, had she been in our place. For that end we must examine and meditate the great virtues which she practised during her life, and particularly, first of all, her lively faith, by which she believed without hesitation the Angel's word, and believed it faithfully and constantly up to the foot of the Cross; secondly, her profound humility, which made her hide herself, hold her peace, submit to every thing, and put herself the last of all; and thirdly, her altogether divine purity, which never has had, and never can have, its equal under heaven; and so on with all her other virtues. Let us remember, I repeat it for the second time, that Mary is the great and exclusive mould of God, proper to make living images of God, at small cost and in a little time; and that a soul which has found that mould, and has lost itself in it, is presently changed into Jesus Christ, whom that mould represents to the life.

• All our Actions *in* Mary

We must do our actions *in* Mary. Thoroughly to understand this practice, we must know, first, that our Blessed Lady is the true terrestrial paradise of the new Adam, and that the ancient Paradise was but a figure of her. There are, then, in this earthly paradise, riches, beauties, rarities, and in-explicable sweetnesses, which Jesus Christ, the new Adam, has left there; it was in this paradise that He took His complacence for nine months, worked His wonders, and displayed His riches with the magnificence of a God. This most holy place is composed only of a virgin and immaculate earth, of which the new Adam was formed, and on which He was nour-ished, without any spot or stain, by the operation of the Holy Ghost, who dwelt there. It is in this earthly paradise that there is the true tree of life, which has borne Jesus Christ, the Fruit of life, and the tree of the knowledge of good and evil, which has given light unto the world. There are in this di-vine place trees planted by the hand of God, and watered by His Divine unction, which have borne and daily bear fruits of a taste divine. There are flower-beds, enamelled with beautiful and various blossoms; virtues, shed-ding odours which embalm the very Angels. There are meadows green with hope, impregnable towers of strength, and the most enticing houses of confidence. It is but the Holy Ghost who can make us know the hidden truth of these figures of material things. There are in this place an air of perfect purity; a fair sun, without the shadow of the Divinity; a fair day, without the night of the Sacred Humanity; a continual burning furnace of love, where all the iron that is cast into it is changed, by excessive heat, to gold. There is a river of humility, which springs from the earth, and which, dividing itself into four branches, waters all that enchanted place; and these are the four cardinal virtues. The Holy Ghost, by the mouth of the Fathers, also styles the Blessed Virgin the Eastern Gate, by which the High-Priest, Jesus Christ, enters the world and leaves it. By it He came the first time, and by it He will come the second.

In the next place, to comprehend thoroughly the practice of doing our actions *in* Mary, we must know that the most holy Virgin is the Sanctuary of the Divinity, the repose of the Most Holy Trinity, the throne of God, the city of God, the altar of God, the temple of God, the world of God. All these different epithets and panegyrics are most substantially true, with reference to the different marvels which the Most High has wrought in Mary. Oh, what riches! what glory! what pleasure! what happiness! to be able to enter in and dwell in Mary, where the Most High has set up the throne of His supreme glory! But how difficult it is for sinners like ourselves to have the permission, the capacity, and the light, to enter into a place so high and so holy, which is guarded not by one of the Cherubim, like the old earthly Paradise, but by the Holy Ghost Himself, who is its absolute master! He Himself has said of it, *Hortus conclusus, soror mea sponsa, hortus conclusus, fons signatus*; Mary is shut, Mary is sealed. The miserable children of Adam and Eve, driven from the earthly Paradise, cannot enter into this one, except by a particular grace of the Holy Ghost, which they ought to merit.

After we have obtained this illustrious grace by our fidelity, we must remain in the fair interior of Mary with complacency, repose there in peace, lean our weight there in confidence, hide ourselves there with assurance, and lose ourselves there without reserve. Thus, in that virginal bosom, the soul shall, first, be nourished with the milk of grace and maternal mercy; secondly, it shall be delivered from its troubles, fears, and scruples; and, thirdly, it shall be in safety against all its enemies,—the world, the devil, and sin,—who never have an entrance there. It is on this account that Mary says that they who work in her shall not sin: *Qui operantur in me, non peccabunt*; that is to say, those who dwell in Mary's spirit shall fall into no considerable fault. Lastly, the soul shall be formed in Jesus Christ, and Jesus Christ in it, because her bosom is, as the holy Fathers say, the chamber of the divine Sacraments, where Jesus Christ and all the elect have been formed.

• All our Actions *for* Mary

Finally, we must do all our actions *for* Mary. As we have given ourselves up entirely to her service, it is but just to do every thing for her, as a servant and a slave. It is not that we can take her for the last end of our services, for that is Jesus Christ alone; but we may take her for our proximate end, our mysterious means, and our easy way to go to Him. Like a good servant and slave, we must not remain idle, but, supported by her protection, we must undertake and achieve great things for this august sovereign. We must defend her privileges when they are disputed; we must stand up for her glory when it is attacked; we must entice all the world, if we can, to her service and to this true and solid devotion; we must speak and cry out against those who abuse her devotion to outrage her Son, and we must at the same time establish this Veritable Devotion; we must pretend to no recompense for our little services, except the honour of belonging to so sweet a Queen, and the happiness of being united by her to Jesus her Son by an indissoluble tie in time and in eternity.

Glory to Jesus in Mary!
Glory to Mary in Jesus!
Glory to God Alone!

"La Comunion," by A. Coutel (1847). Baptistery of the Cathedral of Saint-Sauveur, Aix-en-Provence, France.

CHAPTER 12

Manner of Practicing this Devotion when Receiving Holy Communion

Before Communion

1. You must humble yourself most profoundly before God. **2.** You must renounce your corrupt interior, and your dispositions, however good your own self-love may make them look. **3.** You must renew your consecration by saying, *Tuus totus ego sum, et omnia mea tua sunt,*—I am all thine, my dear Mistress, with all I have. **4.** You must implore that good Mother to lend you her heart, that you may receive her Son there with the same dispositions as her own. You will represent to her that it touches her Son's glory, to be put into a heart so sullied and so inconstant as yours, which would not fail either to lessen His Glory or to destroy it. But if she will come and dwell with you, in order to receive her Son, she can do so by the dominion which she has over all hearts; and her Son will be well received by her, without stains, and without danger of being outraged or destroyed. *Deus in medio ejus, non commovebitur.* You will tell her confidently, that all you have given her of your good is a little matter to honour her; but that by the Holy Communion you wish to make her the same present as the Eternal Father gave her, and that you will honour her more by that than if you gave her all the goods in the world; and, finally, that Jesus, who loves her alone, still desires to take His pleasure and His repose in her, even in your soul, though it be filthier far and poorer than the stable where He made no difficulty to come, simply because she was there. You will ask her for her heart by these tender words: *Accipio te in mea omnia, prœbe mihi cor tuum, O Maria!*

At Communion

On the point of receiving Jesus Christ, after the Our Father, you say three times, *Domine non sum dignus.* Say the first one to the Eternal Father, telling Him you are not worthy, because of your evil thoughts and ingratitudes towards so good a Father, to receive His only Son; but that He is to behold Mary, His handmaid,—*Ecce ancilla Domini,*—who acts for us, and who gives us a singular confidence and hope with His Majesty: *Quoniam singulariter in spe constituisti me.*

You shall say to the Son, *Domine non sum dignus*; telling Him that you are not worthy to receive Him, because of your idle and evil words, and your infidelity to His service; but that nevertheless you pray Him to have pity upon you, that you may introduce Him into the house of His Own Mother, and yours, and that you will not let Him go, without His coming to lodge with her. *Tenui eum, nec dimittam donec introducam illum in domum matris meæ, et in cubiculum genitricis meæ* (Cant. 3, 4). You will pray Him to rise, and come to the place of His repose, and into the ark of His Sanctification: *Surge, Domine, in requiem tuam, tu et arca sanctificationis tuæ.* Tell Him you put no confidence at all in your own merits, your own strength, and your own preparations, as Esau did; but that you trust only in Mary, your dear Mother, as the little Jacob did in the cares of Rebecca. Tell Him that, sinner and Esau as you are, you dare to approach His Sanctity, supported and adorned, as you are, with the virtues of His holy Mother.

You shall say to the Holy Ghost, *Domine non sum dignus*; telling Him that you are not worthy to receive this masterpiece of His charity, because of the lukewarmness and iniquity of your actions, and because of your resistances to His inspirations; but that all your confidence is in Mary, His faithful Spouse. You shall say with St. Bernard, *Hæc mea maxima fiducia, hæc tota ratio spei meæ.* You can pray even Him to come Himself in Mary, His indissoluble Spouse, telling Him that her bosom is as pure, and her heart as burning as ever; and that without His descent into your soul neither Jesus nor Mary will be formed, nor yet worthily lodged.

After Holy Communion

After Holy Communion, while you are inwardly recollected and holding your eyes shut, you will introduce Jesus into the heart of Mary. You will give Him to His Mother, who will receive Him lovingly, will place Him honourably, will adore Him profoundly, will love Him perfectly, will embrace Him closely, and will render to Him, in spirit and in truth, many homages which are unknown to us in our thick darkness. Or else you will keep yourself profoundly humbled in your heart, in the presence of Jesus residing in Mary. Or you will sit like a slave at the gate of the king's palace, where he is speaking with the queen; and while they talk one to the other without need of you, you will go in spirit to heaven and over all the earth, praying all creatures to thank, adore, and love Jesus and Mary in your place: *Venite, adoremus, venite.* Or else you shall yourself ask of Jesus, in union with Mary, the coming of His kingdom on earth, through His holy Mother; or you shall sue for the Divine wisdom, or for Divine love, or for the pardon of your sins, or for some other grace; but always *by* Mary and *in* Mary, saying, while you look aside at yourself, *Ne respicias, Domine, peccata mea,*—"Lord, look not at my sins;" *Sed oculi tui videant æquitates Mariæ,*—"But let your eyes look at nothing in me but the virtues and merits of Mary:" and then, remembering your sins, you shall add, *Inimicus homo hoc fecit,*—"It is I who have committed these sins;" or you shall say, *Ab homine iniquo et doloso erue me*; or else, *Te oportet crescere, me autem minui,*—"My Jesus, you must increase in my soul, and I must decrease; Mary, you must increase within me, and I must be still less than I have been." *Crescite et multiplicamini,*—"O Jesus and Mary, increase in me, and multiply yourselves outside in others also."

There are an infinity of other thoughts which the Holy Ghost furnishes, and will furnish you, if you are thoroughly interior, mortified, and faithful to this grand and sublime devotion which I have been teaching you. But always remember that the more you leave Mary to act in your Communion, the more Jesus will be glorified. The more you leave Mary to act for Jesus, and Jesus to act in Mary, the more profoundly will you humble yourself, and will listen to them in peace and silence, without putting yourself in trouble about seeing, tasting, or feeling; for the just man lives throughout on faith, and particularly in Holy Communion, which is an action of faith. *Justus meus ex fide vivit.*

CHAPTER 13

Consecration of Ourselves to Jesus Christ, the Incarnate Wisdom, by the Hands of Mary

O Eternal and Incarnate Wisdom! O sweetest and most Adorable Jesus! True God and True Man, only Son of the Eternal Father, and of Mary always Virgin! I adore Thee profoundly in the bosom and splendours of Thy Father during eternity; and I adore Thee also in the Virginal bosom of Mary, Thy most worthy Mother, in the time of Thine Incarnation.

I give Thee thanks for that Thou hast annihilated Thyself, in taking the form of a slave, in order to rescue me from the cruel slavery of the devil. I praise and glorify Thee for that Thou hast been pleased to submit Thyself to Mary, Thy holy Mother, in all things, in order to make me Thy faithful slave through her. But, alas! ungrateful and faithless as I have been, I have not kept the promises which I made so solemnly to Thee in my Baptism; I have not fulfilled my obligations; I do not deserve to be called Thy son, nor yet Thy slave; and as there is nothing in me which does not merit Thine anger and Thy repulse, I dare no more come by myself before Thy Most Holy and August Majesty. It is on this account that I have recourse to the intercession of Thy most holy Mother, whom Thou hast given me for a mediatrix with Thee. It is by her means that I hope to obtain of Thee contrition, and the pardon of my sins, the acquisition and the preservation of wisdom. I salute thee, then, O immaculate Mary, living tabernacle of the Divinity, where the Eternal Wisdom willed to be hidden, and to be adored by Angels and by men. I hail thee, O Queen of heaven and earth, to whose empire every thing is subject which is under God.

I salute thee, O sure refuge of sinners, whose mercy fails to no one. Hear the desires which I have of the Divine Wisdom; and for that end, receive the vows and offerings which my lowness presents to thee. I, (name), a faithless sinner, I renew and ratify to-day in thy hands the vows of my Baptism; I renounce for ever Satan, his pomps and works;

and I give myself entirely to Jesus Christ, the Incarnate Wisdom, to carry my cross after Him all the days of my life, and to be more faithful to Him than I have ever been before.

In the presence of all the heavenly court I choose thee this day for my Mother and Mistress. I deliver and consecrate to thee, as thy slave, my body and soul, my goods, both interior and exterior, and even the value of all my good actions, past, present, and future; leaving to you the entire and full right of disposing of me, and all that belongs to me, without exception, according to thy good pleasure, to the greatest glory of God, in time and in eternity.

Receive, O benignant Virgin, this little offering of my slavery, in the honour of, and in union with, that subjection which the Eternal Wisdom deigned to have to thy Maternity, in homage to the power which both of you have over this little worm and miserable sinner, and in thanksgiving for the privileges with which the Holy Trinity hath favoured thee. I protest that I wish henceforth, as thy true slave, to seek thy honour and to obey thee in all things.

O admirable Mother, present me to thy dear Son as His eternal slave, so that as He hath redeemed me by thee, by thee He may receive me. O Mother of mercy, get me the grace to obtain the true Wisdom of God; and for that end put me in the number of those whom thou lovest, whom thou teachest, whom thou conductest, and whom thou nourishest and protectest, as thy children and thy slaves.

O faithful Virgin, make me in all things so perfect a disciple, imitator, and slave of the Incarnate Wisdom, Jesus Christ thy Son, that I may attain, by thy intercession, and by thy example, to the fulness of His age on earth, and of His glory in the heavens.   ***Amen.***

Qui potest capere, capiat.
Quis sapiens, et intelliget hæc?

"Who can receive this, let him receive it.
Who is wise, he will understand these things."

The End

CHAPTER 14

Preparation for Total Consecration to Jesus Christ as a Slave of Love to Mary Most Holy

— By Andrea F. Phillips

Saint Louis de Montfort recommended a period of thirty-three days of preparation for making the Total Consecration to Our Lady. This preparation consists of meditations and prayers suggested by the saint. He explains that, although true devotion is in the heart, outward practices involving the senses engage the whole person, and are powerful aids to the spirit, the memory and the intellect. These practices also serve to edify our neighbor provided they are carried out in a spirit of humility and with the intention of pleasing God alone and advancing our spiritual good.

Saint Louis divided the thirty-three days of preparation into four periods:

Part I: Twelve days in emptying ourselves of the spirit of the world.
Part II: *Week 1* — Knowledge of self.
Part III: *Week 2* — Knowledge of Mary Most Holy.
Part IV: *Week 3* — Knowledge of Our Lord Jesus Christ.

Suggestions for daily practices during the time of preparation:

- Twenty minutes of spiritual reading.
  Topic: the spirit of the world is contrary to the spirit of God.

- Examination of conscience.

- Offering of a small sacrifice to God or some form of personal mortification in reparation for past sins with the intention of countering self-will and practicing purity of heart.

- Pray a decade of the rosary or a full five decades.

- Recite the canticle of Our Lady, the *Magnificat*.

PART I: *Twelve Days*
EMPTYING OURSELVES OF THE SPIRIT OF THE WORLD

> *"If the world hates you, know that*
> *it has hated me before you."* —John 15:18

The spirit of the world is contrary to the spirit of Our Lord Jesus Christ. The spirit of the world consists essentially in the denial of God as creator and supreme ruler. As creator, the triune God created a universe subject to laws, and as supreme ruler He enforces these laws—laws which promote our well-being and eternal good.

The denial of God as creator and supreme ruler is mainly manifested in disobedience, rebellion and sin. This attitude seeks to create a world in which humans—rather than God—make the rules.

Sin: Its Spirit, Its Works and Its "Pomps"

The **spirit of sin** is manifested in the lust of the eyes, and the unlawful desire and pursuit of the pleasures of the flesh; in the pride of possessions and positions; in disobedience to God's laws; and in the abuse of created things. The **works of sin** are all that is produced by disobedience to the Ten Commandments, works that darken the mind, produce error, and seduce, corrupt and weaken the will. The **"pomps" of sin** are the glamour, glitter and charm, which the devil attaches to persons, places and things to render sin alluring, attractive and seductive.

Practices during the initial twelve days: Pray the *Veni Creator Spiritus* and the *Ave Maris Stella* daily.

Recommended reading: The Holy Scriptures, *The Imitation of Christ* by Thomas à Kempis, *The Sinner's Guide* by Luiz de Granada, *The Spiritual Combat* by Dom Lorenzo Scupoli, *Characters of the Passion* by Archbishop Fulton J. Sheen.

PART II: *Week 1*
KNOWLEDGE OF SELF

"You have made us for Yourself, O Lord, and our hearts are restless until they rest in You." —Saint Augustine

During the first week, Saint Louis de Montfort recommends that we employ our prayer and pious actions in asking for knowledge of self. Knowledge of self is essential for knowledge of God.

Narcissism vs. Low Self-Esteem: Both Distance Us from God

Though we are excellent creatures, made to the image and likeness of God Himself, in our fallen state after original sin, we easily take ownership of what was freely given to us: life, senses, talents, appearance, possessions and positions—forgetting their source: God.

Or, on the other extreme, usually because of lack of affirmation or direct abuse, we minimize our true worth, which keeps us from believing that we are immensely loved, and thus trusting in God.

Where the narcissist lacks humility, and tends to think of himself or herself as the ultimate gift to others, the self-doubter misunderstands humility, often compromises his or her personal dignity, and only feels useful when used.

There can also be a combination of both problems.

Reflecting on our contingency and shortcomings helps us to know who we are *not*. Only when we cease to be blinded by our own "greatness" and start to fall out of love with "self," do we get a glimpse of Who God is, and begin to fall in love with Eternal Good.

True self-esteem, the objective appreciation of who we are as creatures and heirs to heaven, counters both self-adoring narcissism and low self-esteem. Both attitudes keep us from seeking our true good and happiness in God, Who is supreme creator, yes, but also a father who has made us heirs to His kingdom—*provided* we want it.

Practices to Help Counter Both Attitudes

For a reality check to the narcissist in us, Saint Louis recommends that we reflect on the fact that, as inheritors of the original sin of Adam and Eve, mankind is naturally inclined to evil. In the "Third Truth" of Part I, Chapter 2, the Saint demonstrates how we are vain and self-centered as peacocks, lazy as snails, groveling as toads, envious as serpents, gluttonous as hogs, and angry as tigers. Or we may choose to reflect on the three considerations of Saint Bernard: that we were made from the slime of the earth, the corruptibility and vulnerability of our present state, and our ultimate end as food of worms.

For low self-esteem and self-doubt, there is nothing better than to reflect on the Crucified, our God giving His life to the last drop of His blood for each of us, and to reflect on His immaculate mother offering Him up for us—indeed, we are that expensive.

There is also nothing more eye-opening and healing than spending time with the Eucharistic Lord in adoration, and developing a personal relationship with Him. Adoration has been called "divine radiation therapy."

Ultimately, in all these reflections, the essential ingredient is honesty: to look at ourselves as we are, and to seek true conversion, and true healing.

Saint Louis says we should pray to the Holy Ghost to enlighten us, and recommends the ejaculations: *"Lord, that I may know Thee!"* or *"Come Holy Ghost."* Another good short prayer: *"Lord, who am I, and Who art Thou?"* Another: *"Jesus, Mary, I trust in Thee."*

Practices for Week 1: Pray the V*eni Creator Spiritus*, the *Ave Maris Stella* and the *Litany of the Holy Ghost* daily.

Recommended reading: The Sacred Scriptures, *The Imitation of Christ* by Thomas à Kempis, *The Sinners Guide* by Luiz de Granada, *The Book of Confidence* by Fr. Thomas de Saint-Laurent, *Abandonment to Divine Providence*, by Jean-Pierre de Caussade, *Introduction to the Devout Life* by Saint Francis de Sales, *Fire Within* by Fr. Thomas Dubay.

PART III: *Week 2*
KNOWLEDGE OF MARY MOST HOLY

"Mary is the sanctuary and the repose of the Holy Trinity, where God dwells more magnificently and more divinely than any other place in the universe..." —Saint Louis de Montfort

The main goal of Saint Louis de Montfort's True Devotion is to seek union *with* Jesus *through* Mary.

Therefore, during the second week of preparation for Total Consecration, Saint Louis directs us to apply all our prayers and works seeking to know the Blessed Virgin Mary, and for this he recommends reflecting on what he has written about Our Lady in this book, all the while invoking the Holy Ghost for knowledge of she who is His spouse. As the Saint says, "...the more He (the Holy Ghost) finds Mary, His dear and indissoluble Spouse, in any soul, the more active and mighty He becomes in producing Jesus Christ in that soul, and that soul in Jesus Christ."

Saint Louis calls Our Lady the "tabernacle of God." Indeed, she is the true ark of the New Covenant. The first ark held the tablets of the law, the second ark held God Himself.

Saint Augustine says that the world was unworthy to receive the Son of God directly from the Father's hands. He was given through Mary so that the world could receive Him through her.

We should make acts of love and thanksgiving toward this creature, immaculate, as befitting the living tabernacle of the True God, free from the original sin that mars us, perfect in her correspondence to God's grace and found worthy to become the mother of the Redeemer.

"She is His (Jesus') mysterious canal; she is His aqueduct, through which He makes His mercies flow gently and abundantly," writes Saint Louis.

In Cana, at Mary's request to alleviate a mere hosting difficulty, Jesus works a stupendous miracle. Noticing that their hosts are out of wine, Our Lady whispers her concern to her Son, who replies that in His eternal will the time is not yet for miracles. But in her trust and union with Him she knows that in His Heart He has said "yes" to her. And she says to the attendants, "Whatsoever he shall say to you, do ye." (John 2:5)

This is her role with Him on our behalf—powerful intercession and sure directive for our lives: "Whatsoever he shall say to you, do ye." She points the way to His Heart, and shows us child-like trust in a God deeply interested even in the details of our lives. This is the faith that works miracles.

We should gratefully think of her as our "Sorrowful Mother," helping to give "birth" to each of us spiritually during the frightful labor of offering her Son for our salvation. We should think of her, amazing in the innocence, fortitude and generosity that allowed her to *stand* at that awful scaffold offering her perfect Son to the Father as the lamb without blemish for our blemishes.

Practices for Week 2: Pray the *Litany of the Holy Ghost* (to which may be added the *Litany of the Blessed Virgin Mary*), the *Ave Maris Stella* and five decades of the *Holy Rosary* daily.

Recommended reading: *The Secret of the Rosary* by Saint Louis Grignion de Montfort, *The Glories of Mary* by Saint Alphonsus de Liguori, *Fatima, a Message More Urgent Than Ever* by Luiz Sergio Solimeo, *The Wonder of Guadalupe* by Francis Johnston, *Saint Bernadette Soubirous* by Abbé François Trochu.

PART IV: *Week 3*
KNOWLEDGE OF OUR LORD JESUS CHRIST

> *"By this hath the charity of God appeared towards*
> *us, because God hath sent his only begotten Son*
> *into the world, that we may live by Him." —*1 John 4:9

In the third week, Saint Louis calls us to apply ourselves to the knowledge of Our Lord Jesus Christ. He recommends that we meditate upon the biblical prefiguring of our Lord's submission to His Blessed Mother in the actions of Jacob and Rebecca. To assist us in the consideration of this mystery, he explains the history of Esau and Jacob as given in chapter 27 of the Book of Genesis and draws out lessons from which we may take spiritual profit. To these considerations the Saint adds the maternal obligations our Blessed Lady incurs on our behalf through the practice of holy slavery and reemphasizes its ultimate aim in the First Truth: "If, then, we establish the solid devotion to our Blessed Lady, it is only to establish more perfectly the devotion to Jesus Christ, and to put forward an easy and secure means for finding Jesus Christ." The contemplation of the Incarnate Word's example in this manner must of necessity bear fruit. Total Consecration to Jesus through Mary is the first and the most perfect of the "external practices" encouraged by Saint Louis de Montfort.

Saint Louis says that if we want to know the mother we must know the Son, for she is the worthy Mother of God. For Our Lord Jesus Christ, true God and true man, is the second person of the Holy Trinity, a divine person with two natures: divine and human.

In an incomprehensible act of love, the second person of the Holy Trinity took on a human nature so as to be able to atone to His Father for the original sin of Adam and Eve and for the sins of humanity. No man, no matter how holy, could have bridged the gap created between God and man by sin. Yet it was only right that humanity atone for the offense. Since only God could sufficiently atone to God, the divine "solution" was a God made man so that as an integral part of humanity, Jesus Christ—God and man— could offer a just return to God.

And here, of course, before this unfathomable divine solution, we go mute and adore this God-made-man before whom "every knee should bow, of those that are in heaven, on earth, and under the earth." (Philippians 2:10)

For this period Saint Louis recommends saying the prayer of Saint Augustine in Part I of the Treatise on True Devotion (page 29), and to say many times a day: "*Lord, that I may know Thee!*" or "*Lord, that I might see Who Thou art!*"

Practices for Week 3: Pray the *Veni Creator Spiritus*, the *Ave Maris Stella*, and the *Litany of the Most Holy Name of Jesus* daily.

Recommended reading: The Sacred Scriptures, *The Imitation of Christ* by Thomas à Kempis, *Christ the Life of the Soul* by Dom Columba Marmion, *Christ in His Mysteries* by Dom Columba Marmion.

INSTRUCTIONS FOR THE DAY OF TOTAL CONSECRATION

At the end of the thirty-three days, Saint Louis entreats us to go to Confession and to receive Holy Communion with the intention of giving ourselves to Jesus Christ in the quality of slaves of love through the hands of Mary. After Holy Communion, which may be made according to the method recommended by the Saint, we should recite the formula of Consecration on pages 121-122. This formula should either be handwritten or printed, but available to be signed as a contract.

Saint Louis also recommends that on the day of Consecration, some offering be made as a tribute to Jesus Christ and Our Blessed Lady, either as a penance for our past unfaithfulness to the vows of our Baptism, or as a testimony of our allegiance to Jesus and Mary as Our Lord and Lady. This offering could take the form of a fast, a personal mortification, a money offering or even a candle, provided it be according to the capacity and means of each, a sincere gift. If a pin is all we can give, Our Lord, Who looks only to the heart's intention, will accept it kindly.

At least once a year, on the anniversary of our Total Consecration, we should renew the same consecration, if possible, observing the same practices during the three weeks.

Saint Louis also recommends that once a month, or even once a day, we renew our consecration by saying the words: "*I am all Thine, and all I have belongs to Thee, O my sweet Jesus, by Mary Thy holy Mother.*"

CHAPTER 15

Prayers Recommended by Saint Louis de Montfort

The young Louis teaches his younger sister how to pray, stained-glass window, Saint-Laurent-sur-Sèvre, France.

MAGNIFICAT

My soul doth magnify the Lord.
And my spirit hath rejoiced in God my Saviour.
Because He hath regarded the humility of His handmaid;
for behold, from henceforth all generations shall call me blessed.
Because He that is mighty hath done great things to me;
and holy is His name.
And His mercy is from generation to generations, to them that fear Him.
He hath showed might in His arm;
He hath scattered the proud in the conceit of their heart.
He hath put down the mighty from their seat;
and hath exalted the humble.
He hath filled the hungry with good things;
and the rich he hath sent empty away.
He hath received Israel His servant, being mindful of His mercy.
As He spoke to our fathers, to Abraham and to his seed forever.   ***Amen.***
Glory be to the Father, etc.

"The Descent of the Holy Ghost,"
watercolor by Dias Tavarez.

VENI CREATOR SPIRITUS

Come, O Creator Spirit blest!
And in our souls take up thy rest;
Come with Thy grace and heavenly aid,
To fill the hearts which Thou hast made.

Great Paraclete! To Thee we cry,
O highest gift of God most high!
O font of life! O fire of love!
And sweet anointing from above.

Thou in Thy sevenfold gifts art known,
The finger of God's hand we own;
The promise of the Father, Thou!
Who dost the tongue with power endow.

Kindle our senses from above,
And make our hearts o'erflow with love;
With patience firm and virtue high
The weakness of our flesh supply.

Far from us drive the foe we dread,
And grant us Thy true peace instead;
So shall we not, with Thee for guide,
Turn from the path of life aside.

Oh, may Thy grace on us bestow
The Father and the Son to know,
And Thee through endless times con-
fessed
Of both the eternal Spirit blest.

All glory while the ages run
Be to the Father and the Son
Who rose from death; the same to Thee,
O Holy Ghost, eternally.   ***Amen.***

LITANY OF THE HOLY GHOST

V/. Lord, have mercy on us.   **R/.** *Christ, have mercy on us.*
V/. Lord, have mercy on us. Christ hear us.
R/. *Christ, graciously hear us.*

Father, all powerful, *have mercy on us.*
Jesus, Eternal Son of the Father, Redeemer of the world, *save us.*
Spirit of the Father and the Son, boundless life of both, *sanctify us.*
Holy Trinity, *hear us.*
Holy Ghost, Who proceedest from the Father and the Son, *enter our hearts.*
Holy Ghost, Who art equal to the Father and the Son, *enter our hearts.*

Promise of God the Father, *have mercy on us.*
Ray of heavenly light, *have mercy on us.*
Author of all good, *have mercy on us.*
Source of heavenly water, *have mercy on us.*
Consuming Fire, *have mercy on us.*
Ardent Charity, *have mercy on us.*
Spiritual unction, *have mercy on us.*

Spirit of love and truth, *have mercy on us.*
Spirit of wisdom and understanding, *have mercy on us.*
Spirit of counsel and fortitude, *have mercy on us.*
Spirit of knowledge and piety, *have mercy on us.*
Spirit of the fear of the Lord, *have mercy on us.*
Spirit of grace and prayer, *have mercy on us.*
Spirit of peace and meekness, *have mercy on us.*
Spirit of modesty and innocence, *have mercy on us.*

Holy Ghost, the Comforter, *have mercy on us.*
Holy Ghost, the Sanctifier, *have mercy on us.*
Holy Ghost, Who governest the Church, *have mercy on us.*
Gift of God, the Most High, *have mercy on us.*
Spirit of the adoption of the children of God, *have mercy on us.*

Holy Ghost, *inspire us with the horror of sin.*
Holy Ghost, *come and renew the face of the earth.*
Holy Ghost, *shed Thy light in our souls.*
Holy Ghost, *engrave Thy law in our hearts.*
Holy Ghost, *inflame us with the flame of Thy love.*
Holy Ghost, *open to us the treasures of Thy graces.*

**Interior of the baldachin showing the Holy Ghost descending in radiant splendor,
St. Peter's Basilica, Rome.**

Holy Ghost, *teach us to pray well.*
Holy Ghost, *enlighten us with Thy heavenly inspirations.*
Holy Ghost, *lead us in the way of salvation.*
Holy Ghost, *grant us the only necessary knowledge.*
Holy Ghost, *inspire in us the practice of good.*
Holy Ghost, *grant us the merits of all virtues.*
Holy Ghost, *make us persevere in justice.*
Holy Ghost, *be Thou our everlasting reward.*

Lamb of God, Who takest away the sins of the world, *send us Thy Holy Ghost.*
Lamb of God, Who takest away the sins of the world, *pour down into our
souls the gifts of the Holy Ghost.*
Lamb of God, Who takest away the sins of the world, *grant us the Spirit of
wisdom and piety.*

V/. Come, Holy Ghost, fill the hearts of Thy faithful.
R/. *And enkindle in them the fire of Thy love.*

Let us pray
Grant, O merciful Father, that Thy Divine Spirit enlighten, inflame and purify
us, that He may penetrate us with His heavenly dew and make us fruitful in
good works; through our Lord Jesus Christ, Thy Son, Who with Thee, in the
unity of the same Spirit, liveth and reigneth forever and ever.   ***Amen.***

**Statue of Mary Star of the Sea,
San Silvestro in Capite, Rome.**

AVE MARIS STELLA

Hail, bright star of ocean,
God's own Mother blest,
Ever sinless Virgin,
Gate of heavenly rest.

Taking that sweet Ave
Which from Gabriel came,
Peace confirm within us,
Changing Eva's name.

Break the captives' fetters,
Light on blindness pour,
All our ills expelling,
Every bliss implore.

Show thyself a Mother;
May the Word Divine,
Born for us thy Infant,
Hear our prayers through thine.

Virgin all excelling,
Mildest of the mild,
Freed from guilt, preserve us,
Pure and undefiled.

Keep our life all spotless,
Make our way secure,
Till we find in Jesus
Joy forevermore.

Through the highest heaven
To the Almighty Three,
Father, Son and Spirit,
One same glory be. ***Amen.***

LITANY OF THE BLESSED VIRGIN MARY

V/. Lord, have mercy on us.   **R/.** *Christ, have mercy on us.*
V/. Lord, have mercy on us. Christ hear us.
R/. *Christ, graciously hear us.*

God the Father of heaven, *have mercy on us.*
God the Son, Redeemer of the world, *have mercy on us.*
God the Holy Ghost, *have mercy on us.*
Holy Trinity, one God, *have mercy on us.*

American TFP Archive

Statue of Mary Help of Christians, Spring Grove, Pennsylvania.

Holy Mary, *pray for us.*
Holy Mother of God, *pray for us.*
Holy Virgin of virgins, *pray for us.*
Mother of Christ, *pray for us.*
Mother of divine grace, *pray for us.*
Mother most pure, *pray for us.*
Mother most chaste, *pray for us.*
Mother inviolate, *pray for us.*
Mother undefiled, *pray for us.*
Mother most amiable, *pray for us.*
Mother most admirable, *pray for us.*
Mother of good counsel, *pray for us.*
Mother of our Creator, *pray for us.*
Mother of our Savior, *pray for us.*
Virgin most prudent, *pray for us.*
Virgin most venerable, *pray for us.*
Virgin most renowned, *pray for us.*
Virgin most powerful, *pray for us.*
Virgin most merciful, *pray for us.*
Virgin most faithful, *pray for us.*
Mirror of justice, *pray for us.*
Seat of wisdom, *pray for us.*
Cause of our joy, *pray for us.*
Spiritual vessel, *pray for us.*
Vessel of honour, *pray for us.*
Singular vessel of devotion, *pray for us.*
Mystical rose, *pray for us.*
Tower of David, *pray for us.*
Tower of ivory, *pray for us.*

House of gold, *pray for us.*
Ark of the covenant, *pray for us.*
Gate of heaven, *pray for us.*
Morning Star, *pray for us.*
Health of the Sick, *pray for us.*
Refuge of sinners, *pray for us.*
Comforter of the afflicted, *pray for us.*
Help of Christians, *pray for us.*
Queen of angels, *pray for us.*
Queen of patriarchs, *pray for us.*
Queen of prophets, *pray for us.*
Queen of Apostles, *pray for us.*
Queen of martyrs, *pray for us.*
Queen of confessors, *pray for us.*
Queen of virgins, *pray for us.*
Queen of all saints, *pray for us.*
Queen conceived without original sin, *pray for us.*
Queen assumed into heaven, *pray for us.*
Queen of the most holy Rosary, *pray for us.*
Queen of peace, *pray for us.*

Lamb of God, Who takest away the sins of world, *spare us, O Lord.*
Lamb of God, Who takest away the sins of the world, *graciously hear us, O Lord.*
Lamb of God, Who takest away the sins of the world, *have mercy on us.*

V/. Pray for us, O holy Mother of God.
R/. *That we may be made worthy of the promises of Christ.*

Let us pray
Grant unto us, Thy servants, we beseech Thee, O Lord God, at all times to enjoy health of soul and body; and by the glorious intercession of Blessed Mary, ever virgin, when freed from the sorrows of this present life, to enter into that joy which hath no end. Through Christ our Lord. **Amen.**

LITANY OF THE HOLY NAME OF JESUS

V/. Lord, have mercy on us.
R/. *Christ, have mercy on us.*
V/. Lord, have mercy on us.
Christ hear us.
R/. *Christ, graciously hear us.*

God the Father of heaven,
have mercy on us.
God the Son, Redeemer of the world,
have mercy on us.
God the Holy Ghost, *have mercy on us.*
Holy Trinity, one God, *have mercy on us.*

Jesus, Son of the living God, *have mercy on us.*
Jesus, splendour of the Father, *have mercy on us.*
Jesus, brightness of eternal light, *have mercy on us.*
Jesus, King of glory, *have mercy on us.*
Jesus, sun of justice, *have mercy on us.*
Jesus, Son of the Virgin Mary, *have mercy on us.*
Jesus, most amiable, *have mercy on us.*
Jesus, most admirable, *have mercy on us.*
Jesus, mighty God, *have mercy on us.*
Jesus, Father of the world to come, *have mercy on us.*
Jesus, angel of the great counsel, *have mercy on us.*
Jesus, most powerful, *have mercy on us.*
Jesus, most patient, *have mercy on us.*
Jesus, most obedient, *have mercy on us.*
Jesus, meek and humble of heart, *have mercy on us.*
Jesus, lover of chastity, *have mercy on us.*
Jesus, lover of us, *have mercy on us.*
Jesus, God of peace, *have mercy on us.*
Jesus, author of life, *have mercy on us.*
Jesus, model of virtues, *have mercy on us.*
Jesus, lover of souls, *have mercy on us.*
Jesus, our God, *have mercy on us.*
Jesus, our refuge, *have mercy on us.*
Jesus, Father of the poor, *have mercy on us.*
Jesus, treasure of the faithful, *have mercy on us.*
Jesus, Good Shepherd, *have mercy on us.*

Jesus, true light, *have mercy on us.*
Jesus, eternal wisdom, *have mercy on us.*
Jesus, infinite goodness, *have mercy on us.*
Jesus, our way and our life, *have mercy on us.*
Jesus, joy of angels, *have mercy on us.*
Jesus, King of patriarchs, *have mercy on us.*
Jesus, master of Apostles, *have mercy on us.*
Jesus, teacher of Evangelists, *have mercy on us.*
Jesus, strength of martyrs, *have mercy on us.*
Jesus, light of confessors, *have mercy on us.*
Jesus, purity of virgins, *have mercy on us.*
Jesus, crown of all saints, *have mercy on us.*

Be merciful, spare us, *O Jesus.*
Be merciful, graciously hear us, *O Jesus.*

From all evil, Jesus, *deliver us.*
From all sin, Jesus, *deliver us.*
From Thy wrath, Jesus, *deliver us.*
From the snares of the devil, Jesus, *deliver us.*
From the spirit of fornication, Jesus, *deliver us.*
From everlasting death, Jesus, *deliver us.*
From the neglect of Thine inspirations, Jesus, *deliver us.*
Through the mystery of Thy holy Incarnation, Jesus, *deliver us.*
Through Thy nativity, Jesus, *deliver us.*
Through Thine infancy, Jesus, *deliver us.*
Through Thy most divine life, Jesus, *deliver us.*
Through Thy labours, Jesus, *deliver us.*
Through Thine agony and Passion, Jesus, *deliver us.*
Through Thy cross and dereliction, Jesus, *deliver us.*
Through Thy sufferings, Jesus, *deliver us.*
Through Thy death and burial, Jesus, *deliver us.*
Through Thy Resurrection, Jesus, *deliver us.*
Through Thine Ascension, Jesus, *deliver us.*
Through Thine institution of the most Holy Eucharist, Jesus, *deliver us.*
Through Thy joys, Jesus, *deliver us.*
Through Thy glory, Jesus, *deliver us.*

Lamb of God, Who takest away the sins of the world, *spare us, O Jesus.*
Lamb of God, Who takest away the sins of the world, *graciously hear us, O Jesus.*

Lamb of God, Who takest away the sins of the world, *have mercy on us, O Jesus.*

V/. Jesus, hear us.
R/. *Jesus, graciously hear us.*

Let us pray
O Lord Jesus Christ, Who hast said: Ask and ye shall receive; seek and ye shall find; knock and it shall be opened unto you; grant, we beseech Thee, to us who ask the gift of Thy divine love, that we may ever love Thee with all our hearts, and in all our words and actions, and never cease praising Thee.

Give us, O Lord, a perpetual fear and love of Thy holy Name; for Thou never failest to govern those whom Thou dost solidly establish in Thy love. Who livest and reignest world without end.   ***Amen.***

MEMORARE BY ST. BERNARD

Remember, O most gracious Virgin Mary, that never was it known that anyone who fled to thy protection, implored thy help, or sought thy intercession was left unaided. Inspired with this confidence, I fly to thee, O Virgin of virgins, my Mother; to thee do I come; before thee I stand, sinful and sorrowful. O Mother of the Word Incarnate, despise not my petitions, but in thy mercy hear and answer me.   ***Amen.***